NASCAR RACERS
TODAY'S TOP DRIVERS

2005 EDITION

NASCAR
LIBRARY COLLECTION

BEN WHITE and **NIGEL KINRADE**

CRESTLINE

CRESTLINE

An imprint of MBI Publishing Company

This edition published in 2005 by Crestline, an imprint of MBI Publishing Company, Galtier Plaza, Suite 200, 380 Jackson Street, St. Paul, MN 55101-3885 USA

Crestline titles are also available at discounts in bulk quantity for industrial or sales-promotional use. For details, please contact: Special Sales Manager at MBI Publishing Company, Galtier Plaza, Suite 200, 380 Jackson Street, St. Paul, MN 55101-3885 USA.

For a free catalog, call 1-800-826-6600, or visit our website at www.motorbooks.com.

ISBN 0-7603-2150-7

On the front cover, top: Kurt Busch, Tony Stewart, Kasey Kahne, Dale Jarrett, Dale Earnhardt Jr. **Bottom:** Terry LaBonte, Michael Waltrip, Jimmie Johnson, Matt Kenseth, Jeff Gordon.

On the back cover, left to right: Tony Stewart, Mark Martin, Jimmie Johnson

Printed in China

CONTENTS

ACKNOWLEDGMENTS

First and foremost, I would like to thank the NASCAR NEXTEL Cup drivers and teams featured in this book for the time they extended to me for this project, as well as past projects in my nearly 20 years of motorsports journalism. Your insights and continued friendship are most appreciated.

A tremendous thanks to Mike Mooney, John Dunlap, Crystal Carraway, Becky Cox, and the entire staff of Nextel for helping to provide information about each driver featured here. Their first season as sponsor of the NASCAR Nextel Cup Series has been both rewarding and exciting.

Hearty thanks to Nigel Kinrade for his fantastic photographs, all of which are so central to this book. Heather Oakley and Lee Klancher of MBI Publishing Company offered tremendous contributions toward making this book a success.

As always, I'd like to thank Mark Ashenfelter, Kenny Bruce, Jon Gunn, Mike Hembree, Jeff Owens, Bob Pockrass, Adam Richardson, Ray Shaw, Whitney Shaw, Kirk Shaw, Steve Waid,

Art Weinstein, and Rea White of *NASCAR Illustrated* and *NASCAR Scene* for their continued friendship and guidance.

Finally, a very sincere thank you to Fred and Priscilla Winecoff—two of my greatest supporters. You are most appreciated.

Brendan Gaughan enjoys his first season racing in the Nextel Cup.

Kurt Busch, NASCAR Nextel Cup champion (97) leads Mark Martin (6) and Rusty Wallace (2) at the Bristol Motor Speedway.

Mark Martin poses as he climbs into his Viagra sponsored Ford.

INTRODUCTION

Few of us get to experience the heart-pounding thrill of pushing a top-of-the-line stock car to its limits around a racetrack. Fewer still possess the elusive combination of skill, courage, and luck that it takes to be a NASCAR winner. As a result, millions of fans around the world look to these favored few as true heroes. So if fate hasn't seen fit to make us NEXTEL Cup champions, then we should at least be able to sit down and chew the fat with our idols of the ovals.

Here we offer an up-close and personal look at the leading stock car drivers of our time. Some have faced both glory in the winner's circle and near-death encounters on the oval over lengthy, perhaps legendary, careers. Others are so young they barely look old enough to drive. Some come to the sport from veritable racing dynasties with winning pedigrees; others emerged from obscure beginnings and fought mightily just for the chance to prove themselves on the track. The highest of triumphs and lowest of disappointments can be seen in the eyes of these men and women, their actions captured by the photographs on these pages.

Wherever they came from and whatever their background, all the men and women who slide through the window into the driver's seat of a NASCAR Nextel Cup car are motivated by the same force: the unrelenting desire to best a rival in a turn or down a straightaway and reach the finish line in front of the rest.

Dale Earhardt Jr. finds himself in trouble in his DEI Chevy.

Matt Kenseth holds up one of his most unique trophys which he won in Las Vegas in March 2004.

GREG BIFFLE

16

Greg Biffle isn't one to be considered flashy or the constant talk of the garage area. He'd rather remain quiet and let his talents on the racetrack to do his talking.

A native of Vancouver, Washington, Biffle has certainly wasted little time making his presence known around NASCAR circles.

While progressing through the various levels of NASCAR racing before making his NASCAR Nextel Cup debut in 2002, his name continued to surface as a contender. But before that huge jump, Biffle logged championships in both the NASCAR Craftsman Truck Series in 2000 and the NASCAR Busch Series in 2002, as well as Rookie of the Year in both divisions. He also ran seven 2002 NASCAR Nextel Cup events for team owners Andy Petree, Jack Roush, and Kyle Petty, gaining experience before his 2003 baptism into the most competitive form of auto racing in the world.

Biffle joined NASCAR's elite circuit in 2003 and, by July, scored a victory in the Pepsi 400 at Daytona International Speedway. That win served as a glimpse of good things to come, since a win in one's rookie season reveals a special talent just waiting to be unleashed. In 2004, he scored a dominant victory in August at Michigan.

Born:	December 23, 1969, Vancouver, Washington
Height:	5-9
Weight:	170 lbs

Sponsor	**Grainger**
Make	**Ford**
Crew Chief	**Doug Richert**
Team	**Jack Roush**

"We've got our team where we need it," Biffle says. "We are capable of winning races and winning a championship. I feel totally confident we'll win another race this season. I'm pretty dang sure of that."

Biffle takes his patriotic No. 16 Roush Racing Ford through its paces.

Biffle listens to advice from his crew chief Doug Richert, a veteran of NASCAR racing since the 1970s.

Team owner Jack Roush gives Biffle a congratulatory hug after one of his many victories. The Vancouver, WA, native quickly adapted to the tracks used in Nextel Cup competition.

NASCAR NEXTEL Cup Career Statistics

YEAR	RACES	WINS	TOP 5S	TOP 10S	POLES	TOTAL POINTS	FINAL STANDING	WINNINGS
2003	35	1	3	6	0	3,696	20th	$2,410,053
2004	36	2	4	8	1	3,902	17th	$3,583,340
TOTALS	71	3	7	14	1	7,598		$5,993,393

JEFF BURTON

30

I n 2004, NASCAR Nextel Cup driver Jeff Burton experienced the biggest change of his 10-year career. Due to the lack of major sponsorship, Burton left the Ford operation owned by Jack Roush in hopes of improving an uncertain future. Though he was reluctant to leave Roush's operation, Burton found some much-needed stability with longtime championship-team owner Richard Childress, who Burton joined forces with in mid-August at Michigan International Speedway.

In high school, Burton excelled at every sport he participated in, following the standard set by his favorite team, the Duke University Blue Devils. As he engaged in some pretty intense go-kart racing, his efforts improved enough to make him a two-time Virginia state champion by the age of seven. By his 17th birthday, Burton was racing the Pure Stock Class at South Boston Speedway, and four years later, he was winning races in dou-

Burton is all smiles just before strapping on his helmet before race time.

ble-digits in the track's premier Late Model Stock division.

Burton's first NASCAR win came at Martinsville, Virginia, in the Busch Series in 1990, and he went on to place 15th in points that season. By 1993, the urge to go on to

Born:	June 29, 1967, South Boston, Virginia	
Height:	5-7	
Weight:	155 lbs	

Sponsor	**AOL Time Warner**
Make	**Chevrolet**
Crew Chief	**Kevin Hamlin**
Team	**Richard Childress**

During a dismal first half of the 2004 season, Burton stands quietly in the garage area contemplating his future.

Winston Cup racing was simply too great to ignore. His first start came on July 11 of that year at New Hampshire International Speedway for team owner Filbert Martocci. Burton ran well in the opening laps, but fell out after crashing on lap 86 of the 300-lap event.

Over time, Burton attracted attention from several prominent team owners, includ-

NASCAR NEXTEL Cup Career Statistics

YEAR	RACES	WINS	TOP 5S	TOP 10S	POLES	TOTAL POINTS	FINAL STANDING	WINNINGS
1993	1	0	0	0	0	52	---	$9,550
1994	30	0	2	3	0	2,726	24th	$594,700
1995	29	0	1	2	0	2,556	32nd	$630,770
1996	30	0	6	12	1	3,539	13th	$884,303
1997	32	3	13	18	0	4,285	4th	$2,296,614
1998	33	2	18	23	0	4,415	5th	$2,626,987
1999	34	6	18	23	0	4,733	5th	$5,725,399
2000	34	4	15	22	0	4,836	3rd	$5,959,439
2001	36	2	8	16	0	4,394	10th	$4,230,737
2002	36	0	5	14	0	4,259	12th	$3,863,220
2003	36	0	3	11	0	4,109	12th	$3,846,884
2004	36	0	2	6	0	3,902	18th	$3,695,070
TOTALS	367	17	91	150	2	43,806		$34,363,673

Jeff Burton leads the pack in his Richard Childress Chevy. Close behind are Bill Elliot (91) and Dale Earnhardt Jr.

ing Bill and Mickey Stavola, as well as Jack Roush, the organization from which all Burton's wins have come. His best season to date was 1999, when he logged six victories, 18 Top 5s, and 23 Top 10s. Burton posted wins that year at Charlotte; both Darlington races; Las Vegas; Rockingham, North Carolina; and the spring race at New Hampshire, where it all began.

Going into the 2005 season, Burton has collected 17 victories since his first start in 1993, but once the team gets back to its winning ways, one can rest assured that he'll add

Burton, in the Roush Racing Ford, makes a pit stop at California Speedway in Fontana, CA.

Jeff Burton behind the wheel of the Chevy he drove for the second half of the 2004 Nextel Cup season.

more triumphs to his personal win column.

"Well, the opportunity to drive for Richard Childress Racing is certainly something that would always interest me for sure," Burton says. "I can tell you this: I feel like I've joined . . . a top-caliber organization that has a chance to win championships and win races, and I feel like I left one that can do the same thing. I do believe that there is time for change. The AOL team is in good shape, and I think I'll come in and do a good job for them. I think, at the end of the day . . . it will be a win for all parties."

Burton wheels the No. 99 Roush Racing Ford just prior to leaving the team to join Richard Childress Racing. Burton scored 17 victories while with the Roush organization.

WARD BURTON

Ward Burton has often been asked why his accent is so different from his younger brother Jeff's. All Ward can do is shrug his shoulders and say, "It's just the way I talk." Ward sounds like a Confederate general—his southern Virginia drawl is as thick and smooth as brown maple syrup. Brother Jeff has it all figured out. When a member of the motorsports media asked Jeff why their accents were so different, Jeff replied, "Well, all I can figure is I was born in the northernmost point of the house and Ward was born in the southern-most part."

In the early 1970s, stock car racing came to the Burton family on the radio every Sunday afternoon. Through the excitement of what he heard over the airwaves, Ward found his all-time sports hero—Winston Cup champion Bobby Allison. Because Allison used No. 12 on most of his cars, Burton claimed the number for his "race cars," the go karts he raced, and even the back of his baseball and football jerseys.

Burton drives his No. 0 Haas Racing Chevrolet low and fast during one of his many outings during the 2004 season.

Like his brother Jeff, Ward began racing go karts at age eight and raced until he was 16 years old. Mini stocks and street stocks appealed to him until late-model stocks caught his eye in 1986. By 1989, Burton earned three victories at South Boston, Virginia, as well as most popular driver honors. He finished second in the Rookie of the Year battle in the NASCAR Busch Series in 1990,

Born: October 25, 1961, South Boston, Virginia

Height: 5-6

Weight: 150 lbs

Sponsor	**NetZero**
Make	**Chevrolet**
Crew Chief	**Bill Ingle**
Team	**Gene Haas**

Burton waits patiently in the sun for the start of the race.

and he eventually won four races in that division, a forum he continues to enter occasionally.

By 1994, Burton found an open door to the NASCAR Winston Cup circuit through team owner A. G. Dillard, the father-in-law of driver Rick Mast. The following year, Burton joined Bill Davis, a successful Arkansas businessman who felt a deep passion for the Winston Cup circuit.

NASCAR NEXTEL Cup Career Statistics

YEAR	RACES	WINS	TOP 5S	TOP 10S	POLES	TOTAL POINTS	FINAL STANDING	WINNINGS
1994	26	0	1	2	1	1,971	35th	$304,700
1995	29	1	3	6	0	2,926	22nd	$634,655
1996	27	0	0	4	1	2,411	33rd	$873,619
1997	31	0	0	7	1	2,987	24th	$1,004,944
1998	33	0	1	5	2	3,352	16th	$1,516,183
1999	34	0	6	16	1	4,062	9th	$2,405,913
2000	34	1	4	17	0	4,152	10th	$2,699,604
2001	36	1	6	10	0	3,846	14th	$3,583,692
2002	36	2	3	8	1	3,362	25th	$4,849,880
2003	36	0	0	4	0	3,550	21st	$3,500,156
2004	34	0	0	3	0	2,929	32nd	$2,471,940
TOTALS	356	5	24	82	7	35,548		$23,845,286

Burton gets a new set of tires at a routine pit stop.

Burton capped 1995 with his first career victory, winning at Rockingham late in the season. From there, he scored wins in the prestigious Southern 500 at Darlington Raceway in the spring of 2000 and summer of 2001.

In 2002, Burton stepped his career up to a new plateau by claiming victory at the season-opening Daytona 500, and the New England 300 at Loudon, New Hampshire, on July 21.

Since those victories, the Bill Davis Racing crew has had many changes, including the departure of crew chief Tommy Baldwin. Over the off-season, Davis worked hard to rebuild

Ward Burton does not yet have a ride for the 2005 Nextel Cup season.

Ward Burton takes his Chevy around the track.

his team and put them back in victory lane, hiring Scott Wimmer as the team's driver. Those wins have not yet come.

With only four races left in the 2003 season, Burton left Davis' operation to join team owner Gene Haas. Crew chief Bill Ingle joined Haas' team in August 2004, and the team started making some impressive finishes.

"Bill and all the guys have been working really hard, and it shows," Burton says. "We've got a good car and a good team, and we want to prove it."

Burton looks deep in thought.

KURT BUSCH

Born: August 4, 1978, Las Vegas, Nevada

Height: 5-11

Weight: 150 lbs

Sponsor	**Rubbermaid**
Make	**Ford**
Crew Chief	**Jimmy Fennig**
Team	**Jack Roush**

When team owner Jack Roush looks for new talent for his powerhouse Roush Racing NASCAR Winston Cup organization, he does so in a very unique way. He used a *Gong Show* style where drivers are invited to audition for rides in his race cars. The best of the group gets further consideration, while the others must retreat back to the lesser-known divisions where they succeeded and excelled.

That was the case with Kurt Busch, one of Roush's current NASCAR Nextel Cup drivers. His audition, so to speak, came in the fall of 1999 when he was eventually placed in a NASCAR Craftsman Truck Series ride. The next season, Busch logged four victories in that division, which paved the way for a stellar career in the prestigious Winston Cup division.

Busch began racing at age 14 in dwarf cars at Pahrump Valley Speedway near Las Vegas and won the division championship in 1995. The next year he won a hobby stock championship, a further step toward becoming a professional racer. Three years passed

Busch takes his No. 97 Roush Racing Ford through a turn at Martinsville (VA) Speedway.

before he became the youngest driver to win a NASCAR Featherlite Southwest Tour title at age 21. That proved to Roush that Busch could win and prompted the longtime team owner to give Busch a chance to show his talents on the bigger high-banked tracks.

Busch moved into the NASCAR Winston Cup ranks in 2000, competing in only seven events so he wouldn't upset his Rookie of the Year bid in 2001. He didn't win rookie honors and struggled with seven DNFs (Did Not Finish) for the season. The biggest blow of the season was his failure to qualify for the final event, then at

Busch tightens his helmet as he sits at the controls of his car just prior to race time.

Atlanta Motor Speedway. Roush recognized the potential that Busch's No. 97 team possessed and made a rather radical move. Roush replaced Busch's entire team with that of fellow Roush driver, Mark Martin, in hopes of giving both teams new life. Veteran crew chief Jimmy Fennig would lead Busch's operation, while Ben Leslie took over the controls of Martin's team.

The switch was perfect. Busch went on to win an incredible four NASCAR Winston Cup races at Bristol, Virginia; Martinsville, Virginia; Hampton, Georgia; and Homestead, Florida. He also went on to finish third in the Winston Cup point standings with 12 Top 5s, 20 Top 10s, and one pole position. Martin's numbers added to one victory, 12 Top 5s, and 22 Top 10s, with a second-place finish in the point standings behind 2002 champion Tony Stewart.

NASCAR NEXTEL Cup Career Statistics

YEAR	RACES	WINS	TOP 5S	TOP 10S	POLES	TOTAL POINTS	FINAL STANDING	WINNINGS
2000	7	0	0	0	0	613	---	$311,915
2001	35	0	3	6	1	3,081	27th	$2,170,630
2002	36	4	12	20	1	4,641	3rd	$3,723,650
2003	36	4	9	14	0	4,150	11th	$5,020,485
2004	36	3	10	21	1	6,506	1st	$4,200,330
TOTALS	150	11	34	61	3	18,991		$15,427,010

Busch (97) leads teammate Mark Martin (6) and Rusty Wallace (2) in a battle for position at Bristol Motor Speedway.

Busch is set for an afternoon of racing just minutes before the green flag. Busch will go on to win the 2004 Nextel Cup.

In the 2003 NASCAR season, Busch's confidence in his abilities to win races and his team's abilities to produce winning race cars couldn't have been higher. He convincingly won events at Bristol, California, Michigan, and Bristol again. In 2004, wins came at Bristol, Tennessee, and Loudon, New Hampshire, through August 22.

The Las Vegas native feels the team is right on track.

"We've had great runs in the past. It's been a process to put the program together to where it is today," Busch says. "I came to the '97 program; it had run for three years and had one Top 5. Having [crew chief] Jimmy Fennig come over in 2002 has really helped the process move along quickly. For us to be championship contenders in 2002 to winning four races that year to four races in 2003, we've won eight races now, and we feel we're an established team and one that can get to victory lane on any given week."

Busch does a burnout after a victory at Bristol Motor Speedway in April 2004.

Busch sits at the rear of his team's transporter during a break in the action.

Busch makes a pit stop for tires and fuel during one of many superspeedway events on the 36-race Nextel Cup schedule.

Busch sits quietly and stares at the inviting race track through the opening of his full-face helmet.

KYLE BUSCH

84

K yle Busch, driver of the Hendrick Motorsports Chevrolet car on the NASCAR Nextel Cup circuit, is working his way into the highest arena of stock car racing with a calculated plan in place. And from the looks of his successes, he is definitely a fast learner.

The younger brother of NASCAR Nextel Cup driver Kurt Busch, Kyle has set his sights on establishing himself quickly. In seven ARCA starts for Hendrick Motorsports, Kyle won twice before his 18th birthday. Of those, he won his first ARCA start at Nashville Speedway and again at Kentucky Speedway. He also scored three pole positions on the ARCA tour.

In 2001, Busch ran six NASCAR Craftsman Truck events for team owner Jack Roush as a

Born:	May 2, 1985, Las Vegas, Nevada
Height:	6-1
Weight:	155 lbs

Sponsor	**Carquest Auto Parts**
Make	**Chevrolet**
Crew Chief	**Lance McGrew**
Team	**Rick Hendrick**

Kyle Busch drives the No. 84 Hendrick Motorsports Chevrolet during a limited Nextel Cup schedule in 2004.

Nineteen-year-old Kyle Busch is all smiles in his new role with Hendrick Motorsports.

Busch studies the job at hand as he sits behind the wheel of his red, white, and blue Chevrolet.

NASCAR NEXTEL Cup Career Statistics

YEAR	RACES	WINS	TOP 5S	TOP 10S	POLES	TOTAL POINTS	FINAL STANDING	WINNINGS
2004	6	0	0	0	0	345	52	$394,489

Busch (left) listens to teammate Jimmie Johnson as he explains a driving maneuver at Lowe's Motor Speedway in Charlotte, NC.

16-year-old high-school junior, with two Top-10 finishes. When he finally joined the NASCAR Busch Series in 2003, he kept everyone on the edges of their seats by finishing second to race winner Matt Kenseth in his debut at Lowe's Motor Speedway in Charlotte, North Carolina.

Busch has run a limited number of NASCAR Nextel Cup events to date and is still looking for big things in what has been called

Busch moves through a turn as he learns the highly competitive Nextel circuit.

Busch smiles as his crew chief, Lance McGrew, chats with his young driver.

the world's most competitive form of auto racing. Few people doubt he will stumble.

"I would have to say Kyle Busch is better than Jeff Gordon was at that age," says team owner Rick Hendrick. "I truly think we're going to see some big accomplishments out of him during his career. After all, he's only 18 years old."

It's easy to smile when Busch thinks of his good fortune with the powerhouse Hendrick Motorsports organization.

DALE EARNHARDT JR.

8

Since first joining the NASCAR Nextel Cup circuit for five events in 1999, Dale Earnhardt Jr., driver of the Dale Earnhardt, Inc. Chevrolet, had enjoyed a tremendous following of fans. Ask him why he has so many fans, and he admits he's quite baffled. Having been on the circuit less than five years and yet to win a championship, Earnhardt Jr. shakes his head and is humbled by the thousands of fans who stand in line for hours just to see him.

When the media scouted the new faces coming into the Winston Cup Series in rookie season, it came as no surprise to find the name "Dale Earnhardt Jr." on their list. What did come as a complete surprise to everybody was that a mere two years later, Earnhardt Jr. would be the only Earnhardt on the circuit.

In the wake of the tragic death of his father at Daytona in February 2001, Earnhardt Jr. was looking to carry on the Earnhardt legacy in NASCAR's premier arena—without his famous father at his side offering advice and encouragement. Throughout the rest of that 2001 season, Earnhardt Jr. was a man everyone looked to for strength.

Early photos of Earnhardt Jr. feature him in one of the black-and-gray pit-crew uniforms of the RCR Enterprises team his father drove for.

Dale Earnhardt Jr. has made his red No. 8 famous among race fans since joining the Nextel Cup circuit full-time in 2000.

Long before he was old enough for a North Carolina driver's license, Earnhardt Jr. had his sights set on becoming a race-car driver just like his dad. He was so serious about this venture that he and his brother Kerry pulled an old 1978 Chevrolet Monte Carlo from the woods and welded roll bars into its stripped interior. Worried that the car wouldn't be safe, Earnhardt Sr. decided to help his young sons and began offering racing advice. Still, he wanted them to work on their own cars to learn the mechanical side of what makes a car go fast.

After a few years campaigning on the short tracks around his Mooresville, North Carolina, home, Earnhardt Jr. was ready to try out the

Born:	October 10, 1974 Kannapolis, North Carolina
Height:	6-0
Weight:	165 lbs

Sponsor	**Budweiser**
Make	**Chevrolet**
Crew Chief	**Tony Eury Jr.**
Team	**DEI**

Earnhardt Jr. enjoys the victory lane celebration after winning the prestigious 2004 Daytona 500.

NASCAR NEXTEL Cup Career Statistics

YEAR	RACES	WINS	TOP 5S	TOP 10S	POLES	TOTAL POINTS	FINAL STANDING	WINNINGS
1999	5	0	0	1	0	500	48th	$162,095
2000	34	2	3	5	2	3,516	16th	$2,801,880
2001	36	3	9	15	2	4,460	8th	$5,827,542
2002	36	2	11	16	2	4,270	11th	$4,570,980
2003	36	2	13	21	0	4,815	3rd	$4,923,497
2004	36	6	16	21	0	6,368	5th	$7,201,380
TOTALS	183	15	52	79	6	23,929		$25,487,374

superspeedways. He earned a Busch Series ride with Dale Earnhardt, Inc. in 1996. He started that first event at Myrtle Beach in seventh position and finished 14th. The powerhouse started by his late father and stepmother, Teresa, in 1995 came to be a racing home for Earnhardt Jr., and he rewarded them with back-to-back Busch Series championships, in his first year and again in 1999.

Earnhardt Jr. parks his Dale Earnhardt, Inc., Chevrolet at the start/finish line after winning the 2004 Daytona 500.

The inevitable rise to what was known as the Winston Cup circuit came in 1999, when Earnhardt Jr. drove in five events. The following year, he competed for Rookie of the Year honors, but fell short to Matt Kenseth by a mere 42 points. When Earnhardt Jr. won his first career Busch Series race in his 16th start, his father was there to celebrate in victory lane. And when he won his first Winston Cup race in April of 2000, his father was there, too, as a competitor. The victory celebration was one to remember. Earnhardt Jr. paid homage to his father one more time by winning "The Winston"

Earnhardt Jr. enjoys a story being told in the garage area by Jimmie Johnson at the far left of the photo.

Earnhardt is often seen wearing his sunglasses and red driver's uniform.

The Dale Earnhardt, Inc., No. 8 crew is lightning fast as they change tires and refuel Earnhardt's famed Chevrolet. Often times, good pit stops have been the key to his wins.

special non-points event for drivers who had won races during the previous season.

In 2001, Earnhardt Jr. achieved three emotional victories. First was the win at Daytona in July, the place of his father's death just a few months earlier. The second win came at Dover in the first NASCAR event after the September 11 terrorist attacks on New York City and Washington, D.C. The third came at Talladega, Alabama, the sight of his father's final career victory.

In late July, Earnhardt Jr. suffered a huge blow to his 2004 NASCAR Nextel Cup efforts when he was involved in a fiery sports car racing accident at Sonoma, California. Even though he was able to avoid missing any races, recovery in the following weeks was very painful.

Earnhardt Jr. has matured into a winning race driver destined for greatness. Like his father before him, his magnificent story will simply continue to unfold.

"We've had our ups and downs, that's for sure," Earnhardt Jr. says. "We certainly will never give up our search for a championship, even though we may have a setback or two. That's always the goal we're shooting for, and one day we'll find it."

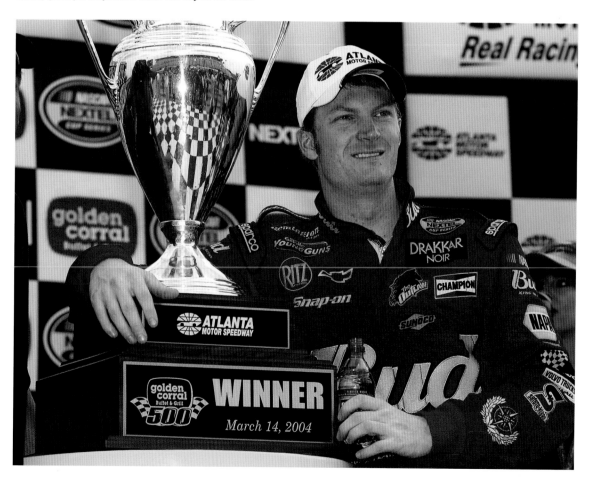

Earnhardt Jr. relaxes after taking the victory at Atlanta Motor Speedway. He admits that Atlanta is one of his favorite tracks.

CARL EDWARDS

99

Ask any NASCAR Nextel Cup driver when they began thinking of a career in the sport, and they will most likely say from a very early age.

Carl Edwards says racing has been part of his life for as long as he can remember. His father, Carl "Mike" Edwards, has been racing modified stock cars and USAC Midgets for 40 years, amassing over 200 victories in the process on several tracks in the Midwest.

The younger Edwards helped his father for many years, working wherever he was needed. That meant changing tires, working on engines, and even driving his transport vehicle to the races. That is until he decided he would try his hand at the same. In Carl's case, he was 13 years old in 1993 when he tried four-cylinder mini-sprints.

After a year of getting used to fast speeds, he won four feature races on tracks around Missouri and Illinois in the mini-sprint series. He gathered 14 more mini-sprint wins over the next two seasons.

In 1997, Edwards showed his talents on dirt tracks in the IMCA modified division. That's where he won Rookie of the Year honors at Capital Speedway in Holt Summit, MO, In 1998.

In 1999, Edwards competed in the modified division and the Dirt Late Model division at Capital Speedway. He enjoyed a string of 13 wins, another rookie title, and the Capital Speedway track championship. It was his

Born:	August 15, 1979
	Columbia, Missouri
Height:	6-3
Weight:	165 lbs

Sponsor	**Roush Racing**
Make	**Ford**
Crew Chief	**Bob Oscborne**
Team	**Roush Racing**

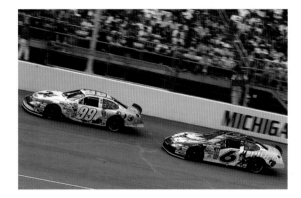

Carl Edwards (99) leads Mark Martin (6).

first taste of NASCAR in their weekly racing series tour.

In 2001, Edwards ran five of seven USAC Silver Crown pavement series events, and by 2002 he had seven starts in the NASCAR Craftsman Truck Series, earning a top-10 at Kansas.

In 2003, Edwards saw his dream come true when he "auditioned" with Roush and was chosen for a spot on the team's multi-driver roster. He immediately became successful with Roush Racing and collected three NASCAR Craftsman Truck Series wins. When NASCAR Nextel Cup driver Jeff Burton left Roush to join team owner Richard Childress, Jack Roush felt the best person to fill the void was Edwards, someone many feel is one of the up-and-coming stars of the sport.

Edwards in his 99 Ford during his first season of Nextel Cup racing.

NASCAR NEXTEL Cup Career Statistics

YEAR	RACES	WINS	TOP 5S	TOP 10S	POLES	TOTAL POINTS	FINAL STANDING	WINNINGS
2004	13	0	1	5	0	1,424	37th	$1,410,570

Edwards gives the fans an up-close-and-personal look at his race car as he zooms by at top speed.

"Well, I think it's gone really well. We've run really well right out of the box and we've had some races where we haven't run so well. At most of the races we had a excuse as to why. There have been weekends where I've been racing the truck the same weekend as the NASCAR Nextel Cup races and I've been going back and forth. I've been getting a little more experience each week. Overall, I feel great about driving for Roush Racing. I'm learning something every week. It's been a huge

Edwards prepares for the race.

A quick pit stop and Edwards is off to finish the race.

learning curve. These guys in NASCAR Nextel Cup racing are really good. I just hope we do well enough to find a sponsor and be able to do it full time next year."

"I always goofed around on trampolines on diving boards and whatever. I saw Tyler Walker do one after he won a World of Outlaws race. I thought to myself, 'Man, that's pretty cool." I tried one of my own and ever since that first one, I've been flipping off the back of my truck each time I win."

Young Carl consults his experienced crew chief Bob Osborne.

BILL ELLIOTT

Bill Elliott enjoyed a new title in 2004 that he had longed for for several years. The title was that of "research driver," meaning he would not run the entire NASCAR Nextel Cup circuit but rather be available for the occasional race where team owner Ray Evernham would try something slightly different and not risk valuable and precious

Born: October 8, 1955, Dawsonville, Georgia

Height: 6-1

Weight: 185 lbs

Sponsor	**Dodge Dealers**
Make	**Dodge**
Crew Chief	**Ray Evernham**
Team	**Ray Evernham**

NASCAR NEXTEL Cup Career Statistics

YEAR	RACES	WINS	TOP 5S	TOP 10S	POLES	TOTAL POINTS	FINAL STANDING	WINNINGS
1976	7	0	0	0	0	556	49th	$11,635
1977	10	0	0	2	0	1,002	36th	$20,575
1978	10	0	0	5	0	1,176	34th	$42,065
1979	14	0	1	5	0	1,709	28th	$57,450
1980	11	0	0	4	0	1,232	35th	$42,545
1981	13	0	1	7	1	1,442	31st	$70,320
1982	21	0	8	9	1	2,718	25th	$226,780
1983	30	1	12	22	0	4,279	3rd	$479,965
1984	30	3	13	24	4	4,377	3rd	$660,226
1985	28	11	16	18	11	4,191	2nd	$2,433,187
1986	29	2	8	16	4	3,844	4th	$1,069,142
1987	29	6	16	20	8	4,202	2nd	$1,619,210
1988	29	6	15	22	6	4,488	1st	$1,574,639
1989	29	3	8	14	2	3,774	6th	$854,570
1990	29	1	12	16	2	3,999	4th	$1,090,730
1991	29	1	6	12	2	3,535	11th	$705,605
1992	29	5	14	17	2	4,068	2nd	$1,692,381
1993	30	0	6	15	2	3,774	8th	$955,859
1994	31	1	6	12	1	3,617	10th	$936,779
1995	31	0	4	11	2	3,746	8th	$996,816
1996	24	0	0	6	0	2,627	30th	$716,506
1997	32	0	5	14	1	3,836	8th	$1,607,827
1998	32	0	0	5	0	3,305	18th	$1,618,421
1999	34	0	1	2	0	3,246	21st	$1,624,101
2000	32	0	3	7	0	3,267	21st	$2,580,823
2001	36	1	5	9	2	3,824	15th	$3,618,017
2002	36	2	6	13	4	4,158	13th	$3,753,490
2003	36	1	9	12	0	4,303	9th	$4,321,185
2004	6	0	0	1	0	595	38th	$567,900
TOTALS	737	44	175	320	55	90,890		$35,948,749

Bill Elliott pits at the very end of pit road in California.
Frequently that helps a driver get back on track the fastest.

NASCAR Nextel Cup championship points. He is now running a handful of races and loving every minute of his "part-time" season in 2004.

A victory for the Georgia native late in the 2001 season at Homestead, Florida—the 41st win of his career—ended a six-year winless streak. When the checkered flag fell over his Ray Evernham–owned Dodge, it silenced the critics who claimed that Elliott was simply too old to find victory lane again.

During a Nextel Cup event at Daytona in July 2004, Elliott entered his own Dodge and sported the number *98*. Elliott finished in the top-10.

Bill Elliot in his No.91 ride.

But Elliott wasn't finished. In 2002, he won pole position at Pocono, Pennsylvania, and Loudon, New Hampshire, in back-to-back efforts and continued that good fortune with a win at Pocono and the prestigious Brickyard 400 at Indianapolis Motor Speedway the next week.

Stock car racing has been all the redhead from Georgia has ever known. He and his brothers Ernie and Dan got started early, scrounging around their father's junkyard and fixing up old cars that were perfect for racing—racing around the dirt roads between junk piles, that is. The boys of George and Mildred Elliott had found their calling.

With George acting as an early sponsor and financier, the fledgling race team spent summer weekends competing on small dirt tracks. The brothers eventually persuaded their father to buy a Winston Cup machine, a beat-up old Ford Torino purchased from Bobby Allison. The boys first raced the car at Rockingham, North Carolina, on February 29, 1976, with Bill finishing 33rd in his

Winston Cup debut. Still, the boys felt rich with the $640 in prize money they collected.

They struggled mightily for the next few years and threatened more than once to close the doors on the team for good. Thankfully, businessman Harry Melling entered the picture and provided the Elliotts with top-notch equipment, and the wins began to come.

The first victory finally came in the last race of the 1983 season at Riverside, California, young Elliott's 117th career start. He posted three more wins in 1984 to set the stage for an incredible 1985 season. Bill won 11 races in 28 starts, starting his assault by dominating the Daytona 500. He won at Atlanta and Darlington, and overwhelmed the competition at Talladega in May, winning the pole position with a speed of 202.398 miles per hour. He broke an oil line during the race, but made up five miles under green conditions by turning lap after lap at more than 205 miles per hour, regaining the lost deficit to win the race.

The come-from-behind victory at Talladega

Elliott (91) leads Kurt Busch (97) in a Nextel Cup event in 2004. Elliott campaigned a limited schedule after decades of running the full schedule.

was his second win of the four major NASCAR events. To win three meant he would be awarded a $1 million bonus from series sponsor R.J. Reynolds. Elliott suffered brake problems at the next $1 million–eligible event at Charlotte, but came back at Darlington to win the Southern 500 and the bonus in its inaugural year.

In August 1987, Elliott turned the fastest time in a stock car, reaching 212.809 miles per hour at Talladega. He was crowned (then) Winston Cup champion in 1988. From 1995 to 2000, Elliott again fielded his own cars with co-owner Charles Hardy, but the two never could break into the winner's circle. When Elliott joined Evernham at the start of the 2001 season, veteran motorsports writers were predicting them to win multiple races and billed

them as a dream team of sorts. The strings of multiple wins haven't come, but Elliott did prove that he could still win races.

Elliott now races whenever he can find sponsorship or the team wants to try something slightly different in hopes of benefiting the championship-caliber machines of Kasey Kahne and Jeremy Mayfield. Elliott doesn't mind his new role one bit.

"I've been blessed with a great career over the years, but this is where I want to be," Elliott says. "A limited schedule with Ray [Evernham] is perfectly fine with me. I'm really very happy with this arrangement."

Elliott's No. 91 Evernham Motorsports Dodge has become familiar to his millions of fans. It has become his number since running a limited schedule.

BRENDAN GAUGHAN

77

Born:	July 10, 1975, Las Vegas, Nevada
Height:	5-9
Weight:	190 lbs

Sponsor	Kodak
Make	Dodge
Crew Chief	Shane Wilson
Team	Roger Penske

One could say that January 6, 2004 was one of the best days in the life of Brendan Gaughan, driver of the Penske Racing Dodge. It was the day when the announcement was made that he would be driving for one of the most powerful and most respected team owners in all of motorsports. It was his fourth-place finish in the 2003 NASCAR Craftsman Truck Series championship that helped ice the deal.

In that series that year, Gaughan won six events and led the series point standings for eight consecutive weeks heading into the season finale. He ultimately finished 29th after being caught up in an accident with 33 laps remaining, ending his championship bid. Still, his season-long efforts were enough to impress Penske, as well as long-time veteran and former NASCAR champion Rusty Wallace. The fact that he had been crowned the 2000 and 2001 NASCAR Grand National division champion and Winston West Series champion proved to Penske and Wallace that Gaughan knew how to win championships.

Gaughan's first season as a rookie in NASCAR Nextel Cup competition has had its ups and downs and has been a classroom on wheels. The vast majority of his finishes were

Gaughan makes a pit stop during the 2004 Nextel Cup season.

measured in double digits, but he did log a sixth-place finish at Fontana, California, in June 2004.

"The difference in competition at this level versus another, like the truck series, is the number of cars capable of running in a tight pack," Gaughan has learned. "With the NASCAR Truck Series, there might have been 10 to 15 trucks weekly that I knew I was competing against. The rest of the teams gave it all they had, but some weeks it still wasn't good enough.

"At this level, there are more than 37 cars, and some weeks, the entire field of 43. Everyone is running within 1/100th of a second from one another and it is dog-eat-dog. Anyone who thinks they can just jump into a Cup car and hit the circuit needs a brake check. Drivers at this level have been competing in NASCAR divisions for years, and only a few are ever lucky enough to make it to the top."

Brendan Gaughan proudly displays the colors on his No. 77 Penske Racing Dodge.

NASCAR NEXTEL Cup Career Statistics

YEAR	RACES	WINS	TOP 5S	TOP 10S	POLES	TOTAL POINTS	FINAL STANDING	WINNINGS
2004	36	0	1	4	0	3,165	28th	$2,929,400

JEFF GORDON

24

Not since "The King" Richard Petty first showed up on the NASCAR grids in 1958 has such a young driver shown, and gone on to fulfill, such overwhelming promise as Jeff Gordon. By the time he was 30 years old, Gordon had four Winston Cup titles under his belt—the third driver ever to win that many—and he is widely considered the man most likely to break Petty's record of seven championships. With his good looks and astounding success, Gordon has established himself as a household name to both veteran fans and schoolchildren alike.

Gordon showed his talent early. The Vallejo, California, native began his racing career at age five in quarter midgets and go karts. Over the next 15 years, awards and

records fell to Gordon like dominos in every mode of open-wheel short-track racing.

When he was still a teenager, Gordon garnered offers from prestigious teams in several forms of auto racing, including one from former

Jeff Gordon (24) is a blur as he enjoys a winning 2004 Nextel Cup season.

Born: August 4, 1971, Vallejo, California
Height: 5-7
Weight: 150 lbs

Sponsor	**DuPont**
Make	**Chevrolet**
Crew Chief	**Robbie Loomis**
Team	**Rick Hendrick**

Gordon raises his arms in celebration in victory lane, a place he has frequently visited since joining the circuit full-time in 1993.

Formula One world champion Jackie Stewart. In the end, Gordon chose stock cars.

He attended the Buck Baker Driving School in early 1990 and simply loved the experience. With pillows stuffed inside a seat clearly too big for him, Gordon quickly got a handle on the heavier, bulkier stock cars and was turning some impressive times by the end of the day.

In his first year in the Busch Series division, Gordon won 1991 Rookie of the Year honors driving for owner Bill Davis. In 1992, he

NASCAR NEXTEL Cup Career Statistics

YEAR	RACES	WINS	TOP 5S	TOP 10S	POLES	TOTAL POINTS	FINAL STANDING	WINNINGS
1992	1	0	0	0	0	70	---	$6,285
1993	30	0	7	11	1	3,447	14th	$765,168
1994	31	2	7	14	1	3,776	8th	$1,779,523
1995	31	7	17	23	8	4,614	1st	$4,347,343
1996	31	10	21	24	5	4,620	2nd	$3,428,485
1997	32	10	22	23	1	4,710	1st	$6,375,658
1998	33	13	26	28	7	5,328	1st	$9,306,584
1999	34	7	18	21	7	4,620	6th	$5,858,633
2000	34	3	11	22	3	4,361	9th	$3,001,144
2001	36	6	18	24	6	5,112	1st	$10,879,757
2002	36	3	13	20	3	4,607	4th	$4,981,170
2003	36	3	15	20	4	4,785	4th	$5,107,762
2004	36	5	16	25	6	6,490	3rd	$6,437,660
TOTALS	401	69	191	255	52	56,540		$62,275,172

Gordon's paint scheme changed in 2001 from a rainbow design to flames. He won the 2001 championship with the new paint style and is always red hot on all types of race tracks.

Gordon's crew, led by crew chief Robbie Loomis, makes a pit stop for the four-time Nextel Cup champion.

won 11 Busch Series pole positions and scored three victories. When he was ready to make his Winston Cup debut at the final event of the 1992 season at Atlanta, he had to get written permission from his parents, since he was not yet 21 years old. He finished unremarkably, in 31st place, but his career soon took off after being signed to a Winston Cup contract by owner Rick Hendrick for the 1993 season.

Gordon established himself in the NASCAR Winston Cup ranks in immediate fashion. He was named Rookie of the Year in 1993 and earned the distinction of becoming the youngest driver to win a 125-mile qualifying race at Daytona International Speedway.

Gordon started his 1994 season by winning the Busch Clash, a special non-points event. He grabbed his first Winston Cup win at the Coca-Cola 600 at Charlotte Motor Speedway in May, and followed that with a victory in the Brickyard 400 at Indianapolis Motor Speedway in August, making him the first stock car driver to grace Indy's coveted victory circle.

Gordon answers questions from various media outlets outside of his Hendrick Motorsports hauler.

Gordon's young-looking face can be seen as he sits behind the controls of his No. 24 Hendrick Motorsports Chevrolet.

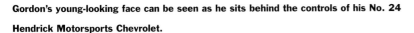

Gordon is always available to sign autographs for his fans.

In 1995, only his third full season, Gordon accomplished the unthinkable by winning the Winston Cup championship over the likes of Dale Earnhardt, Terry Labonte, and Rusty Wallace. He was the youngest Winston Cup champion in the modern era (since 1972) and the second youngest ever (1950 NASCAR champion Bill Rexford was only a few months younger). Gordon went on to collect further NASCAR Nextel Cup championships in 1997, 1998, and 2001 to become the winningest active driver.

Over the past couple of seasons, Gordon has struggled to get back to championship form. If mechanical problems didn't haunt him, it was constantly being caught up in someone else's misfortune on the racetrack.

With victories in 2004 at Talladega; Fontana, California; Sonoma, California; Daytona, and Indianapolis, Gordon and company have clearly proven they are back on the championship track.

"It's just so much fun going to the racetracks when you know that you've got a chance at winning, just pretty much every weekend you feel like you've got some kind of a shot at it," Gordon says. "You know, the guys, they're together, the chemistry's there, the communication's there, the momentum's there. I mean, things just feel really, really good."

ROBBY GORDON

31

There's no doubt Robby Gordon, driver of the RCR Enterprises Chevrolet, likes to race virtually anything on wheels. Like so many who began their careers in motorsports other than stock car racing, Gordon didn't grow up driving Chevrolets, Dodges, or Fords, but off-road championship machines beginning in 1985.

The Orange, California, native wasted little time making a name for himself. He became the overall winner of the Baja 1,000 in 1987 and 1989 and also won the Mickey Thompson Stadium Series championships in 1988 and 1989.

In 1991, Gordon began racing in the IMSA road-race series for longtime NASCAR Winston Cup team owner Jack Roush. Gordon became a four-time winner of the 24 Hours of Daytona in the IMSA GTS class in four consecutive years, all for Roush Racing. That led to the open-wheel Indy Car machines for his first full season in 1993, driving for the legendary A. J. Foyt.

Beginning in the early 1990s, Gordon was also busy wheeling NASCAR machines on limited schedules for such legendary team owners as Junie Donlavey, Robert Yates, Felix Sabates, and

Robbie Gordon (31) put his Richard Childress–owned Chevrolet through its paces during the 2004 Nextel Cup season.

even the late Dale Earnhardt, to name a few.

By 1996, the bug returned for more off-road racing, and he logged four wins and the SCORE Off-Road Trophy Truck championship.

Gordon survived one of his most frightening accidents in the 1997 Indianapolis 500 after qualifying 12th. On the 19th lap, fire broke out in the cockpit of his car, and he suffered second- and third-degree burns on his hands, wrist, and right

Born: January 2, 1969, Cerritos, California
Height: 5-10
Weight: 180 lbs

Sponsor	**Cingular**
Make	**Chevrolet**
Crew Chief	**Chris Andrews**
Team	**Richard Childress**

Gordon, shown in the cockpit ready to go, often drives a variety of race cars, including open-wheel Indy cars.

thigh. The injuries sidelined him for a month. He came back for two more seasons, one of which was with a team he owned himself, before directing his attention to NASCAR Winston Cup racing.

In November 2001, Gordon logged his first career victory at Loudon, New Hampshire, while driving in 10 events for team owner Richard Childress. He joined Childress full-time in 2002 and was winless that first full season, but scored victories on the road courses at Sonoma, California, and Watkins Glen, New York, in 2003.

In 2004, Gordon challenged for wins from February through August but could not capture a victory. Still, there's no mistaking the competitive style he brings to the racetrack each week.

"We all want to win races, because that's what it's all about," Gordon says. "That applies in every form of racing in the world. So all you can do is your best and hope a win will come."

NASCAR NEXTEL Cup Career Statistics

YEAR	RACES	WINS	TOP 5S	TOP 10S	POLES	TOTAL POINTS	FINAL STANDING	WINNINGS
1991	2	0	0	0	0	---	55th	$27,265
1993	1	0	0	0	0	---	94th	$17,665
1994	1	0	0	0	0	---	76th	$7,965
1996	3	0	0	0	1	---	57th	$32,915
1997	20	0	1	1	0	---	40th	$622,439
1998	1	0	0	0	0	---	67th	$24,765
2000	17	0	1	2	0	---	43rd	$620,781
2001	17	1	0	3	0	---	44th	$1,371,900
2002	36	0	1	5	0	---	20th	$917,020
2003	36	2	4	10	0	3,856	16th	$3,705,320
2004	36	0	2	6	0	3,646	23rd	$4,025,550
TOTALS	170	3	11	27	1	7,502		$11,373,585

BOBBY HAMILTON JR.

32

Born:	January 8, 1978, Nashville, Tennessee
Height:	5-5
Weight:	170 lbs

Sponsor	**Cal Wells**
Make	**Chevrolet**
Crew Chief	**Harold Holly**
Owner	**PPC Racing**

Since his birth on January 8, 1978, Bobby Hamilton Jr. has known very little except the exciting world of stock car racing. But the Nashville, Tennessee native isn't complaining. He has enjoyed a successful winning career and has now moved to NASCAR's highest arena, the Nextel Cup circuit.

His father, Bobby Hamilton Sr., drove short tracks around Tennessee himself for many years until given the chance drive in NASCAR Nextel Cup competition during the making of the movie "Days of Thunder" in 1989. From there, Hamilton Sr. began a NASCAR Nextel Cup career (then known as the NASCAR Winston Cup) where he logged four-career victories.

Hamilton Sr., is now a fixture on the NASCAR Craftsman Series tour. Hamilton, Jr. has followed his father on the Nextel Cup circuit, driving for team owner Cal Wells in the No. 32 PPI Racing Chevrolet.

In 1997, the career of Hamilton Jr. began when his father bought him a 1971 Ford Pinto for race competition. The two quickly transformed the small compact car into a powerful racing machine that served as tool for the beginning of a successful career for the young rising star.

With that memorable first car, Hamilton Jr. started racing in the mini-modified division at Highland Rim Speedway near Ridgetop, Virginia. A year later, he was the driver taking home the trophy as the track's season champion.

In 1998, Hamilton Jr. moved up to ARCA Supercar Series where he notched four top-five finishes in just five starts in the Superspeedway series.

With his father watching closely and offering advice where needed, he tested the waters of the NASCAR Busch Series that same fall in 1998 at Rockingham and Atlanta. Two years later, midway through the 2000 season, Hamilton, Jr. got the opportunity to race full-time in the Busch Series while driving for team owner Dave Carroll.

In a surprise move in 2001, Hamilton made 10 starts in NASCAR Nextel Cup competition, seven coming with team owner Larry McClure and three with former owner Andy Petree.

Hamilton Jr. captured his first Busch Series win in 2002 at New Hampshire, setting the stage for a remarkable 2003 season. That year, Hamilton won four times, coming at Chicago, Memphis, Kentucky and Phoenix and finished fourth in the series point standings while driving for Rensi Motorsports and team owners Ed Rensi, Sam Rensi and Gary Weisbaum.

In 2004, Hamilton left the Rensi operation to take advantage of another shot at NASCAR Nextel Cup racing. During a period of re-organization within the Hickory, N.C. based team, driver Ricky Craven was released and some personnel reassigned. Part of that massive change came with Hamilton, Jr. being placed behind the controls as well as the hiring of crew chief Harold Holly.

In an abbreviated 2004 schedule after joining Wells' organization late into the season, Hamilton Jr. struggled with some race tracks that were new to him and failed to score a top-10 finish. Still, both Hamilton and Holly are being billed as a possible winning force in 2005, having done so together in the NASCAR Busch Series together.

"It's been a big learning curve," Hamilton Jr. said of his ememergence into NASCAR Nextel Cup racing. "The finishes speak for themselves. We've had decent finishes and some that were way back in the final finishing order. It's been up and down. It's frustrating. You're trying to pin point every little thing that there is but there's just not enough time and practice to get everything you need.

"It's a totally different animal from the NASCAR Busch series. Over there, you can take two or three smart people who can help you kick tail all year long. Over here, you've got to have all the pieces of the puzzle in place going in. The driver has to know everything about the race track and you've almost got to be in a Cup car for a couple of years to get that feel. It can be so confusing. You're constantly thinking of everything in the world, asking yourself, 'How can I pick up a second or a half-second. It's been a real big roller coaster and it's also a ton of pressure trying to come in here and put together something productive."

Bobby Hamilton Jr. in his No. 32 Tide Chevrolet.

NASCAR NEXTEL Cup Career Statistics

YEAR	RACES	WINS	TOP 5S	TOP 10S	POLES	TOTAL POINTS	FINAL STANDING	WINNINGS
2004	17	0	0	0	0	1,271	39th	$1,259,210

KEVIN HARVICK

29

Today, Kevin Harvick is a household name in NASCAR Nextel Cup racing. But that wasn't the case until the tragic, untimely death of Dale Earnhardt in 2001, which changed everything.

Only a Hollywood screenwriter could have dreamed up Kevin Harvick's seemingly unbelievable debut in Winston Cup racing that year. When the season began, Harvick was just a second-year Busch Series driver for Richard Childress, a year removed from being named Busch Series Rookie of the Year in 2000. By the end of 2001, Harvick had two Nextel Cup victories, the Winston Cup 2001 Rookie of the Year, and the Busch Series championship under his seatbelt.

Harvick's rise was so surprising because no one could have foreseen the fate of Childress' top driver, legendary seven-time champion Earnhardt. After the black day of February 18, 2001, when Earnhardt was killed on the final lap of the Daytona 500, Childress

Born:	December 8, 1975, Bakersfield, California
Height:	5-10
Weight:	175 lbs

Sponsor	**GM Goodwrench**
Make	**Chevrolet**
Crew Chief	**Todd Berrier**
Team	**Richard Childress**

Harvick is often seen smiling as he visits with his crew and his fans in the garage area.

turned to his new young talent to wheel his Winston Cup cars.

Harvick was quick to make an impact. He scored a photo-finish victory over Jeff Gordon in his third career start, coming at Atlanta only two weeks after Earnhardt's death. Despite the hectic cross-country schedule, Harvick campaigned in both of what were then the Winston Cup and Busch Series divisions simultaneously. The effort paid off. Harvick not only went on to notch a second big-league triumph, at the inaugural Winston Cup event at Chicago, but he also posted several Busch Series races en route to that division's 2001 championship. Counting a NASCAR Craftsman Truck Series event, Harvick entered 70 races in three different series during his remarkable year.

Kevin Harvick (29) began driving the No. 29 Richard Childress Racing Chevrolet in 2001 after the death of seven-time champion Dale Earnhardt Sr.

NASCAR NEXTEL Cup Career Statistics

YEAR	RACES	WINS	TOP 5S	TOP 10S	POLES	TOTAL POINTS	FINAL STANDING	WINNINGS
2001	35	2	6	16	0	4,406	9th	$4,302,202
2002	35	1	5	8	1	3,501	21st	$3,748,100
2003	36	1	11	18	1	4,770	5th	$4,994,249
2004	36	0	5	14	0	4,228	14th	$4,739,010
TOTALS	142	4	27	56	2	16,905		$17,783,561

Harvick (29) leads Bobby Labonte (18) and Tony Stewart (20) into turn one.

The biggest victory of his career came in the 2003 Brickyard 400 at Indianapolis Motor Speedway. It was just another example of his continued growth as a competitor, which may someday translate into joining that list of NASCAR champions. All told, the Bakersfield, California, native has four career NASCAR Winston Cup wins to his credit.

Harvick struggled to find victory lane in 2004 but still managed to remain in the Top 10 in the NASCAR Nextel Cup point standings for

Harvick is one of the up-and-coming stars of Nextel Cup racing and is destined to win a championship in the future.

Harvick's crew surrounds his black and silver machine to give him the fastest service possible. Note the small number *3* just behind his door number in honor of the late Dale Earnhardt.

the majority of the 11-month season.

"This is a race team that's been really consistent," Harvick says. "We've made some mistakes this year, and for some reason we just haven't been one of those win-a-lot-of-races race team. We've been in position the end of last year and even this year, but we just haven't capitalized on it. It's not that we haven't put ourselves in position; we just haven't capitalized on a lot of situations. We all want to win, but it's just hard to put it all together."

Harvick drives his machine low in hopes of turning a fast time. Over the past four years, he has made the No. 29 famous.

DALE JARRETT

88

Throughout the 2004 NASCAR Nextel Cup season, Dale Jarrett, driver of the Robert Yates Racing Ford, showed he wouldn't give up his championship hopes. Consistent Top-5 finishes eluded him for much of the season, but with only a couple of months to go to complete the season, a Top-10 birth into the new Chase for the Championship program wasn't out of the question.

He learned his never-give-up attitude from his famous father, Ned Jarrett, a two-time NASCAR Grand National champion in his own right, who taught young Dale that the journey could be long and hard and unpredictable.

Dale Jarrett leads Rusty Wallace (2) on the concrete surface of Martinsville (VA) Speedway.

Born:	November 26, 1956, Conover, North Carolina
Height:	6-2
Weight:	215 lbs

Sponsor	**UPS**
Make	**Ford**
Crew Chief	**Mike Ford**
Team	**Robert Yates**

Jarrett relaxes while dressed in the brown-and-yellow colors of UPS, his primary sponsor.

The younger Jarrett wasted little time experiencing that for himself. He started racing in 1977 at Hickory Motor Speedway in the Limited Sportsman Division before jumping over to the Busch Series when it started in 1982. He launched his Winston Cup career in 1984 during a one-race ride with former driver and team owner Emmanuel Zervakis at Martinsville, Virginia. He started 24th, finished 14th, and collected $1,515 for his first Winston Cup start.

NASCAR NEXTEL Cup Career Statistics

YEAR	RACES	WINS	TOP 5S	TOP 10S	POLES	TOTAL POINTS	FINAL STANDING	WINNINGS
1984	3	0	0	0	0	267	---	$7,345
1986	1	0	0	0	0	76	---	$990
1987	24	0	0	2	0	2,177	25th	$143,405
1988	29	0	0	1	0	2,622	23rd	$118,640
1989	29	0	2	5	0	2,789	24th	$232,317
1990	24	0	1	7	0	2,558	25th	$214,495
1991	29	1	3	8	0	3,124	17th	$444,256
1992	29	0	2	8	0	3,251	19th	$418,648
1993	30	1	13	18	0	4,000	4th	$1,242,394
1994	30	1	4	9	0	3,298	16th	$881,754
1995	31	1	9	14	1	3,584	13th	$1,363,158
1996	31	4	17	21	2	4,568	3rd	$2,985,418
1997	32	7	20	23	3	4,696	2nd	$3,240,542
1998	33	3	19	22	2	4,619	3rd	$4,019,657
1999	34	4	24	29	0	5,262	1st	$6,649,596
2000	34	2	15	24	3	4,684	4th	$5,984,475
2001	36	4	12	19	4	4,612	5th	$5,366,242
2002	36	2	10	18	1	4,415	9th	$3,935,670
2003	36	1	1	7	0	3,358	26th	$4,055,487
2004	36	0	6	14	0	4,214	15th	$4,539,330
TOTALS	567	31	158	249	16	68,174		$45,843,819

Jarrett (88) leads Derrike Cope (50), Michael Waltrip (15), Mark Martin (6), and Casey Mears (41) as they battle for position.

A variety of team owners called on Jarrett to wheel their cars before Cale Yarborough included him in his retirement plans of 1989. Jarrett was to split the schedule with the three-time Winston Cup champion. At the conclusion of that season, however, Yarborough brought in a new driver, and Jarrett found himself without a ride. Fortunately, the search for a new team didn't last long.

When Neil Bonnett, driver of the Wood Brothers Ford, was injured in a crash at Darlington in 1990, Jarrett was tapped to fill

Jarrett shows some intensity as he waits for his crew to service his car in the garage area.

Jarrett shows rookie Brian Vickers (25) how to drive low in a corner.

Jarrett, the son of two-time NASCAR champion Ned Jarrett, is a 20-year veteran and champion himself. His championship came in 1999.

the void, presumably for just a race or two. Bonnett's injuries required a lengthy recovery period, however, and Jarrett was put in the driver's seat for the duration of the season.

In August 1991, Jarrett captured his first career Winston Cup win after battling head-to-head with Davey Allison at Michigan International Speedway, beating the late Alabama driver to the finish line by a foot.

The next year, Jarrett left Wood Brothers to join the untested Joe Gibbs organization, a move that sparked much criticism. Jarrett brought the team to prominence with a victory over Dale Earnhardt in the 1993 Daytona 500.

Jarrett was again called upon to fill in after Ernie Irvan was gravely injured in an accident during a practice session at Michigan International Speedway in August 1994. Jarrett was released from his contract with Gibbs and took over Irvan's place with the Robert Yates team for the 1995 season.

Despite questions about whether he was experienced enough to take on such a potent ride, Jarrett quickly silenced the critics, winning at Pocono in July and finishing in the Top 10 in 14 of 31 races that year. When Irvan miraculously returned for the full season in 1996, Jarrett moved to a second Yates Ford team with crew chief Todd Parrott at the helm. The results were nothing short of dominant.

In 1996, Jarrett won the Daytona 500, the Coca-Cola 600 at Charlotte, the Brickyard 400 at Indianapolis, and the Miller 400 at Brooklyn, Michigan. After a season-long bid for the Winston Cup championship, Jarrett finished a close third behind Terry Labonte and Jeff Gordon.

Three years later, Jarrett finally added that elusive jewel to his crown by claiming the 1999 NASCAR Winston Cup championship with Robert Yates Racing.

Jarrett won at Rockingham, North Carolina, in February 2003, but since that trip to victory lane, very few positives have come to the Conover, North Carolina, native. He's been around the sport long enough to know that winners go through slumps from time to time and eventually return to prominence.

In 2004, Jarrett did log a third at Michigan in June, a third at Chicago in July, and a second at Indianapolis in August. Even though the Top-10 bid was hard fought, he still considers it a good season.

"The amount of effort that's been put forth by Robert Yates Racing is just incredible," Jarrett says. "I know everybody out here works hard, but I know what happens at Robert Yates Racing. Even though some of the results over the past year and a half haven't shown what we've been doing, I think now we're starting to show that those efforts were worthwhile."

JIMMIE JOHNSON

At the start of the 2002 NASCAR Winston Cup season, drivers, team owners, and pit crews once again formed new associations. Among those new associations was rookie driver Jimmie Johnson and team owners Rick Hendrick and four-time NASCAR Winston Cup champion Jeff Gordon. When Johnson fired his engine for the first time during Speedweeks at Daytona in February of last year, there were no bands playing or fireworks exploding in the distance. Johnson was just another driver looking to make his mark on the ultra-competitive NASCAR Winston Cup circuit. Even though his blue-and-silver Chevrolet Monte Carlo carried the required rookie stripes on its back bumper, the man behind the controls seemed anything but a competitor in his freshman season. It

Born:	September 17, 1975, El Cajon, California
Height:	5-11
Weight:	175 lbs

Sponsor	**Lowe's Home Improvement**
Make	**Chevrolet**
Crew Chief	**Chad Knaus**
Team	**Rick Hendrick**

Jimmie Johnson proudly displays his team's colors through the turns at Bristol Motor Speedway.

Johnson peeks out from behind his helmet as he prepares to exit his Hendrick Motorsports Chevrolet.

helped that he had Hendrick Motorsports equipment under him and Gordon, the winner of 61 Winston Cup races, offering support and advice.

Johnson showed he had enough talent to be considered for the ride. One could say Johnson came straight out of the desert to join the ranks of the NASCAR elite. From go karts to off-road racing, he won six racing championships and three Rookie of the Year titles. Off-road racing deeply appealed to Johnson, but with Chevrolet's decision to cease funding for the series, he began to think of racing in other forms of motorsports. He once wanted to drive Indy Cars, but stock cars had always been a favorite, even though stock car racing was more prominent on the East Coast, which was thousands of miles away.

He moved from his El Cajon, California, home and headed east in hopes of starting to

NASCAR NEXTEL Cup Career Statistics

YEAR	RACES	WINS	TOP 5S	TOP 10S	POLES	TOTAL POINTS	FINAL STANDING	WINNINGS
2001	3	0	0	0	0	213	---	$122,320
2002	36	3	6	21	5	4,600	5th	$2,847,700
2003	36	3	14	20	2	4,932	2nd	$5,517,850
2004	36	8	20	23	1	6,498	2nd	$5,692,620
TOTALS	111	14	40	64	80	16,240		$14,180,490

Johnson gets left-side service from his crew during a crucial pit stop. His Chad Knaus–led Hendrick Motorsports crew is known for getting off of pit road in record time.

climb NASCAR's ladder. In 1998, he started three NASCAR Busch Series events and a year later added two more to his schedule. In 2000, Johnson campaigned full-time in the NASCAR Busch Series in a bid for rookie honors. Even though he finished third in the rookie battle, he did finish 10th in the season-long point standings after starting 31 events. In 2001, Johnson scored his first win in a stock car in the inaugural Busch Series event at Chicagoland Speedway in Joliet, Illinois. Along with the win came four Top 5s and nine Top 10s and an eighth-place finish in the point standings.

Crew chief Chad Knaus, left, and Johnson stand in the garage area and study the television monitors a during a practice session.

Johnson leads a tightly bunched field stacked behind him. It isn't uncommon to see his Hendrick Motorsports Chevrolet out front.

Johnson sits quietly for a moment almost as if he is posing for a studio shot.

Johnson is all smiles as he raises the winner's trophy at Darlington (SC) Raceway in spring 2004.

Hendrick and Gordon saw something in Johnson and offered him a contract as a NASCAR Winston Cup driver. The team owner and driver had so much confidence in him that they signed him before the start of the 2001 season and allowed him to fulfill his Busch Series commitment that year. The final piece of the puzzle was the hiring of Chad Knaus as the team's crew chief. Knaus had worked with Gordon as a crew member and had shown that he had the leadership skills to operate the race team in winning fashion. He and Johnson proved to be a strong and viable combination. In 2002, Johnson exceeded all expectations. He won three NASCAR Winston Cup events at Fontana, California, and was twice a winner at Dover, Delaware. He logged four pole positions as well as six Top 5s and 21 Top 10s. Even though he fell short of Winston Cup Rookie of the Year, which went to Ryan Newman, it was still a remarkable season.

Johnson was just as strong in 2003, winning races at Charlotte in May and New Hampshire in July and September, respectively. And in 2004, he won convincingly at Darlington in April, Charlotte in May, Pocono in June, and Pocono again in August. For the majority of the season, he led the NASCAR Nextel Cup points championship standings.

Johnson knows exactly why he's in the championship hunt each season.

"I think being in the situation I'm in—driving the Hendrick Motorsports cars—is what has put me in that position," Johnson says. "From the competitive side, the first two or three races are the key ones to be doing that. Luckily we've been able to finish well at Daytona and Rockingham and Atlanta or Vegas after that. Just being in great equipment—stuff that doesn't fall apart and that's competitive."

KASEY KAHNE

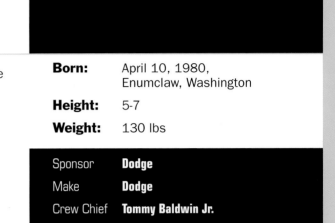

9

Born:	April 10, 1980, Enumclaw, Washington
Height:	5-7
Weight:	130 lbs

Sponsor	**Dodge**
Make	**Dodge**
Crew Chief	**Tommy Baldwin Jr.**
Team	**Ray Evernham**

Throughout the 2004 NASCAR Nextel Cup season, rookie sensation Kasey Kahne certainly wasted no time touting his name as a future superstar in NASCAR Nextel Cup competition. He didn't stand atop his Evernham Motorsports Dodge and shout about his stellar talent. Instead, he elected to use his right foot and precision feel to place his solid-red Dodge in position to win in many of the 36 races that make up the schedule.

Ever since Jeff Gordon barnstormed onto NASCAR during the final event of what was then known as the NASCAR Winston Cup circuit in 1992, most every team owner in the sport had expressed an interest in the drivers who cut their teeth in the open-wheel sprint-car ranks. The reason is that Gordon developed his stellar driving abilities there,

setting the stage for 69 career victories through the August 8 Brickyard 400 at Indianapolis and four NASCAR championships coming in 1995, 1997, 1998, and 2001, respectively.

So when Ray Evernham, owner of Evernham Motorsports, happened to catch a race at The Dirt Track at Lowe's Motor Speedway some three seasons ago, he saw a driver he liked very much, another racing phenom some called a carbon copy of Gordon.

That driver's name is Kasey Kahne, an open-wheel ace who followed a career path much like that of Gordon's.

Kahne's open-wheel sprint-car efforts were financed by his family. He also accepted an offer from open-wheel team owner Steve Lewis who,

with team manager Bob East, is credited with helping Gordon and Tony Stewart become stars.

That led to two years in the NASCAR Busch Series, serving as the foundation for his present NASCAR Nextel Cup efforts.

Evernham knew he had found a diamond the rough.

Today, Kahne, driver of the No. 9 Evernham Motorsports Dodge, is a rising star within the NASCAR arena and admits he's enjoying his rookie season of Nextel Cup competition.

In only one season, Kahne had seven Top-5 finishes through August, including four second-place finishes. With just slightly more luck to his credit, those second-place runs could be counted as four victories

Soft-spoken and quiet, Kahne often looks intense when he's around the racetracks.

"I look serious a lot because I am, but really I'm having a lot of fun, especially inside," Kahne says. "I enjoy what I'm doing. So far I'd say what's great is knowing we can run up front and we can compete for wins. Every week it seems like we have a shot at running in the Top 10, and that's what's been great so far this season driving for Ray Evernham and Dodge. The other stuff, there really hasn't been too much stuff that hasn't been good. Just having more things to do, getting pulled in more directions, really at times it's like I wish I didn't have to do all this stuff, but other than that it's all been pretty good."

Kasey Kahne drives the Ray Evernham Motorsports Dodge in 2004, a front-running machine driven by veteran Bill Elliott in 2003. Kahne drives as if he is a veteran himself.

NASCAR NEXTEL Cup Career Statistics

YEAR	RACES	WINS	TOP 5S	TOP 10S	POLES	TOTAL POINTS	FINAL STANDING	WINNINGS
2004	36	0	13	14	4	4,274	13	$4,759,020

MATT KENSETH

17

Now that the 2003 NASCAR season has ended, Matt Kenseth, driver of the Roush Racing Ford and Madison, Wisconsin, native has a new title to add to his list of accomplishments. He's now a champion in NASCAR competition.

Kenseth gained the points lead in March 2003 after his win at Las Vegas and held it for the remainder of the 36-race season. Further, he did so with numbers so far ahead of the second-place finisher that he would have had to sit out several races for anyone to have caught up.

Kenseth's driving career began when his father bought a race car and had his son maintain it with a few friends who helped on the crew. Once Matt reached his 16th birthday, his dad gave him the car. He progressed to the ARTGO Series and became its youngest winner (besting Winston Cup driver Mark Martin for that honor).

A large part of getting into the Winston Cup arena is getting noticed. Kenseth was hired by Jack Roush for the full 2000 Winston Cup season after five races with Roush in 1999. The young driver shocked the racing community by winning the Coca-Cola World 600 at Lowe's Motor Speedway in May that year.

Matt Kenseth (17) leads Kevin Harvick (29) and teammate Kurt Busch (97) as they race for position.

His 14th-place finish in the points standings was good enough to bring Kenseth the Rookie of the Year award in 2000.

After a winless 2001 campaign, Kenseth quickly asserted himself at the front of the pack in 2002. He claimed victory at Rockingham, North Carolina, in the second race of the season, captured another check-

Born: March 10, 1972, Madison, Wisconsin
Height: 5-9
Weight: 152 lbs

Sponsor	**DeWalt Tools**
Make	**Ford**
Crew Chief	**Robbie Reiser**
Team	**Jack Roush**

Kenseth is intense, possibly thinking of the chassis set-up his Roush Racing crew has put underneath him.

ered flag at Texas Motor Speedway in April, and added a third trophy to the shelf with a win at Michigan in June. Kenseth also scored victories at Richmond, Virginia, in September and Phoenix, Arizona, in November to become the winningest driver of the season.

The 2004 NASCAR Nextel Cup season proved to be a bit more of a challenge as far as wins go, having collected two wins early in the season at Rockingham, North Carolina, and Las Vegas. Still, Kenseth was consistently in the Top 10 in the NASCAR Nextel Cup standings.

"I'm awfully proud of this team, and it's an honor to drive for all these guys," Kenseth says. "They put their hearts in this stuff, and they give me some great race cars, especially today and last week—every week."

NASCAR NEXTEL Cup Career Statistics

YEAR	RACES	WINS	TOP 5S	TOP 10S	POLES	TOTAL POINTS	FINAL STANDING	WINNINGS
1998	1	0	0	1	0	150	---	$42,340
1999	5	0	1	1	0	434	29th	$143,561
2000	34	1	4	11	0	3,711	14th	$2,408,138
2001	36	0	4	9	0	3,982	13th	$2,565,579
2002	36	5	11	19	1	4,432	8th	$3,888,850
2003	36	1	11	25	0	5,022	1st	$4,038,124
2004	36	2	8	16	0	6,069	8th	$6,223,890
TOTALS	184	9	39	82	1	23,800		$19,310,482

BOBBY LABONTE

18

Quiet and determined, Bobby Labonte, driver of the Joe Gibbs Racing Chevrolets, is clearly on top of his game. His talent is coupled with that of crew chief Michael "Fatback" McSwaim and race cars that routinely go to the front. Labonte enjoyed consistently good finishes at the beginning of the 2003 season, but this pattern didn't continue through the close of the season.

From all he's accomplished, it seems that Labonte was born to be a stock car racer. Back in 1984, a shy and rather young Bobby could be found over and underneath the Chevrolets that his older brother Terry would drive. That year, the elder Labonte captured his first NASCAR Winston Cup championship. While Terry was accepting the trophy and all the checks, Bobby's mental wheels began turning toward putting his own racing career in motion.

Even before Terry's glory days with team owner Billy Hagan, Bobby followed in his brother's footsteps by fielding a quarter-midget racer at the mere age of five. In 1987,m Bobby secured his own Late Model Sportsman career, where he won the track championship at Caraway Speedway with 12 victories and seven pole positions in 23 races.

He finished fourth in the season-long point standings in 1990, and came back in 1991 to win the NASCAR Busch Series championship.

By 1993, Bobby found a home with Bill Davis Racing but lost Rookie of the Year honors to future Winston Cup champion Jeff Gordon. Having finished 19th and 21st in the point standings in his first two full seasons, Labonte was happy to take the ride with Joe Gibbs Racing when Dale Jarrett vacated the spot to join Robert Yates in 1995. Labonte won three races that season and set the stage for good things ahead. Since the beginning of Labonte's union with the former coach of the NFL's Washington Redskins, record-breaking performances have been the standard for the team from Huntersville, North Carolina.

Born:	May 8, 1964, Corpus Christi, Texas
Height:	5-9
Weight:	175 lbs

Sponsor	**Interstate Batteries**
Make	**Pontiac**
Crew Chief	**Michael McSwain**
Team	**Joe Gibbs**

Labonte finished a strong second in the 1999 point standings and came back to win his own NASCAR Winston Cup championship in 2000. He collected four victories, including a win in the prestigious Brickyard 400 in his title year.

In 2002 and 2003, Labonte logged a total of three victories and hoped to improve that in 2004. Unfortunately, no wins came. Since the Fontana, California, event in June, he has consistently made his mark in the Top 10 in points.

Labonte is ready for another title.

"I know everyone shows up at the beginning of the season with dreams of a championship, but after having the opportunity to enjoy it, it makes me want it that much more. Of course, we have goals of winning races and pole positions, but our main goal is to be back at the top of the heap and let everyone take their best shot as us."

NASCAR NEXTEL Cup Career Statistics

YEAR	RACES	WINS	TOP 5S	TOP 10S	POLES	TOTAL POINTS	FINAL STANDING	WINNINGS
1992	2	0	0	0	0	110	---	$8,350
1993	30	0	0	6	1	3,221	19th	$395,660
1994	31	0	1	2	0	3,038	21st	$550,305
1995	31	3	7	14	2	3,718	10th	$1,413,682
1996	31	1	5	14	4	3,590	11th	$1,475,196
1997	32	1	9	18	3	4,101	7th	$2,217,999
1998	33	2	11	18	3	4,180	6th	$2,980,052
1999	34	5	23	26	5	5,061	2nd	$4,763,615
2000	34	4	19	24	2	5,130	1st	$7,361,386
2001	36	2	9	20	1	4,561	6th	$4,786,779
2002	36	1	5	7	0	3,810	16th	$3,851,770
2003	36	2	12	17	4	4,377	8th	$4,745,258
2004	36	0	5	11	1	4,277	12th	$4,570,540
TOTALS	402	21	106	177	26	49,174		$39,120,592

Bobby Labonte No. 18, in his Chevy during the 2004 Nextel Cup season.

TERRY LABONTE

5

A two-time NASCAR Winston Cup champion, Terry Labonte, driver of the Hendrick Motorsports Chevrolet, has performed on a variety of track configurations, but he would admit his career of late has been a roller-coaster ride. Still, after 23 years of highs and lows, the 45-year-old Texan challenges the young guns in his drive for another championship.

Labonte's career began when team owner Billy Hagan picked him to drive his NASCAR Nextel Cup cars when Terry was only 22 years

Born: November 16, 1956, Corpus Christi, Texas

Height: 5-10

Weight: 165 lbs

Sponsor	**Kellogg's**
Make	**Chevrolet**
Crew Chief	**Jim Long**
Team	**Rick Hendrick**

NASCAR NEXTEL Cup Career Statistics

YEAR	RACES	WINS	TOP 5S	TOP 10S	POLES	TOTAL POINTS	FINAL STANDING	WINNINGS
1978	5	0	1	3	0	659	39th	$20,545
1979	31	0	2	13	0	3,615	10th	$130,057
1980	31	1	6	16	0	3,766	8th	$215,889
1981	31	0	8	17	2	4,052	4th	$334,987
1982	30	0	17	21	2	4,211	3rd	$363,970
1983	30	1	11	20	3	4,004	5th	$362,790
1984	30	2	17	24	2	4,508	1st	$713,010
1985	28	1	8	17	4	3,683	7th	$694,510
1986	29	1	5	10	1	3,473	12th	$522,235
1987	29	1	13	22	4	4,002	3rd	$825,369
1988	29	1	11	18	1	4,007	4th	$950,781
1989	29	2	9	11	0	3,564	10th	$704,806
1990	29	0	4	9	0	3,371	15th	$450,230
1991	29	0	1	7	1	3,024	18th	$348,898
1992	29	0	4	16	0	3,674	8th	$600,381
1993	30	0	0	10	0	3,280	18th	$531,717
1994	31	3	6	14	0	3,876	7th	$1,125,921
1995	31	3	14	17	1	4,146	6th	$1,558,659
1996	31	2	21	24	4	4,657	1st	$4,030,648
1997	32	1	8	20	0	4,177	6th	$2,270,144
1998	33	1	5	15	0	3,901	9th	$2,054,163
1999	34	1	1	7	0	3,580	12th	$2,475,365
2000	32	0	3	6	1	3,433	17th	$2,239,716
2001	36	0	1	3	0	3,280	23rd	$3,011,901
2002	36	0	1	4	0	3,417	24th	$3,143,990
2003	36	1	4	9	1	4,162	10th	$3,643,695
2004	36	0	0	6	0	3,519	26th	$3,745,240
TOTALS	817	22	181	359	27	99,041		$37,069,617

Terry Labonte takes the "Tony the Tiger" cereal figure for a ride in his Hendrick Motorsports Chevrolet. Kellogg's has been his primary sponsor for over a decade.

old and working as a crew member for Hagan. Labonte took over for Dick May in a race at Dover, Delaware, in September and brought Hagan's No. 92 Chevy home 10th. He also started five events in 1978, finishing in the Top 10 three times, including a fourth place at Darlington Raceway in South Carolina, in his first career Winston Cup start. The Texas oil-man had found his star. Although seat time was what Labonte needed most, sharing races with May allowed him to keep his rookie status for the following season.

Labonte and Hagan ditched the No. 92 for No. 44 at the start of the 1979 season, and solid, consistent finishes followed. Labonte made 31 starts that year and netted a 10th-place finish in the Winston Cup point

Labonte pulls into his pit as his crew converges over his No. 5 machine. In both 2005 and 2006 he will cut back to a limited schedule, running 10 races each season.

standings. He fell just a few spots behind a young driver named Dale Earnhardt in the 1979 Rookie of the Year chase.

Labonte's love affair with Darlington continued at the 1980 Southern 500, where he collected his first Winston Cup victory—a win that still ranks among the biggest upsets in the race's history. Leaders David Pearson and Dale Earnhardt hit an oil slick in turn one, caused by Frank Warren's blown engine. Labonte trailed two seconds behind and won the race under caution.

Labonte is ready for action as he is strapped into his Hendrick Motorsports Chevrolet, waiting for the command to fire his engine.

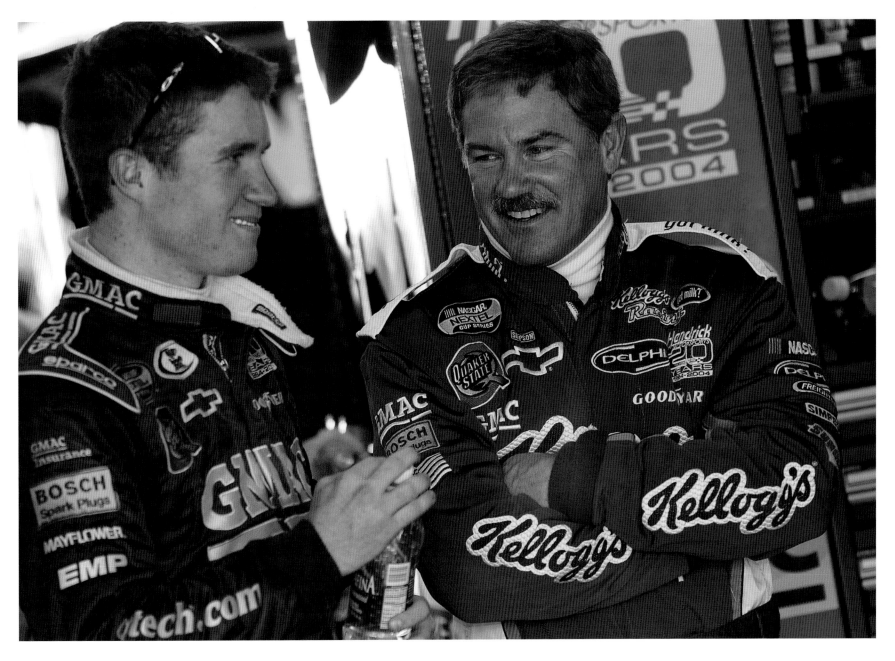

Rookie driver Brian Vickers (left) enjoys a laugh with his teammate, Labonte. Years earlier, Labonte took Vickers to school each morning, as they lived in the same neighborhood.

The consistency continued, and in 1984 Labonte gave Hagan his only Winston Cup championship to date. From the outside, it looked as though relations between the champion driver and team owner were at an all-time high, but in the shadows, problems loomed. By 1987, Labonte moved over to Junior Johnson's organization, then one of the top teams on the tour. Limited success came with Johnson through 1989, as was the case with owner Richard Jackson in 1990. A surprise reunion with Hagan came in 1991, and the renewed partnership lasted through 1993. Following his 1984 title run, Labonte claimed only six victories over the next nine seasons, none of them with Jackson or Hagan.

Just as the critics turned up the assault, saying that Labonte was on the downhill slide—that glory had passed him by—an unexpected turn of events gave new life to his career. Ricky Rudd departed Hendrick Motorsports to start his own Winston Cup organization. Labonte's name surfaced as a possible replacement, and a strong finish at North Wilkesboro in late 1993 convinced team owner Rick Hendrick that Labonte was his man. The union with Hendrick has produced more victories for Labonte (eight) than with any other team owner, and led to a second Winston Cup title in 1996.

The pace slowed down after the second championship, with just one win per season from 1997 to 1999, and a winless 2000 and 2001. But Labonte continues on with Hendrick

Motorsports, and the team feels confident in its potential for further success.

By the spring of 2003, Labonte started to make some progress, and he was getting some good finishes. The most special was winning the prestigious Southern 500 at Darlington, South Carolina, on August 31, 2003.

Labonte struggled to find victory lane in 2004 but still considered it a good season.

"We have a great race team at Hendrick Motorsports," Labonte says. "It may not show by being in victory lane each week, but we do have runs we're very proud of. Now we just need another win to add to the list. We have performances at times that are better than what the end result reads."

STERLING MARLIN

After nearly three decades of racing in NASCAR, Sterling Marlin, driver of the Chip Ganassi Racing Dodge, has never let fame and success taint his easygoing country personality.

The sound of race engines roaring and welders crackling has filled Marlin's ears for as long as he can remember. Racing is a way of life for Sterling, just as it was for his dad, Clifton "Coo Coo" Marlin. Throughout Sterling's

Born: June 30, 1957, Columbia, Tennessee

Height: 6-0

Weight: 180 lbs

Sponsor	**Coors Light**
Make	**Dodge**
Crew Chief	**Tony Glover**
Team	**Chip Ganassi**

Sterling Marlin has been a fixture in NASCAR racing since his father, Clifton "Coo Coo" Marlin raced in the 1970s. Here he is shown in his familiar silver Ganassi Racing Dodge.

NASCAR NEXTEL Cup Career Statistics

YEAR	RACES	WINS	TOP 5S	TOP 10S	POLES	TOTAL POINTS	FINAL STANDING	WINNINGS
1976	1	0	0	0	0	76	---	$565
1978	2	0	0	1	0	226	---	$10,170
1979	1	0	0	0	0	123	---	$505
1980	5	0	0	2	0	588	42nd	$29,810
1981	2	0	0	0	0	164	---	$1,955
1982	1	0	0	0	0	94	---	$4,015
1983	30	0	0	1	0	2,980	19th	$143,564
1984	14	0	0	2	0	1,207	37th	$54,355
1985	8	0	0	0	0	721	37th	$31,155
1986	10	0	2	4	0	989	36th	$113,070
1987	29	0	4	8	0	3,386	11th	$306,412
1988	29	0	6	13	0	3,621	10th	$521,464
1989	29	0	4	13	0	3,422	12th	$473,267
1990	29	0	5	10	0	3,387	14th	$369,167
1991	29	0	7	16	2	3,839	7th	$633,690
1992	29	0	6	13	5	3,603	10th	$649,048
1993	30	0	1	8	0	3,355	15th	$628,835
1994	31	1	5	11	1	3,443	14th	$1,127,683
1995	31	3	9	22	1	4,361	4th	$2,253,502
1996	31	2	5	10	0	3,682	8th	$1,588,425
1997	32	0	2	6	0	2,954	25th	$1,301,370
1998	32	0	0	6	0	3,530	13th	$1,350,161
1999	34	0	2	5	1	3,397	16th	$1,797,416
2000	34	0	1	7	0	3,363	19th	$1,992,301
2001	36	2	12	20	1	4,741	3rd	$4,517,634
2002	29	2	8	14	2	3,703	18th	$3,711,150
2003	36	0	0	11	0	3,745	18th	$3,960,809
2004	36	0	3	7	0	3,857	21st	$4,117,750
TOTALS	640	10	82	210	13	72,557		$31,689,248

formative years, there was always some kind of stock car in the shed out back.

At the age of 15, Marlin helped on his dad's pit crew during the summer, and the underage driver occasionally took the wheel of the transporter on the long trips from Columbia, Tennessee, to places like Michigan, Daytona, or Texas. When school was in session, Marlin worked on his dad's cars but stayed home to play football.

Marlin soon got the chance to fulfill his dream of driving stock cars. With help from his father's Winston Cup sponsor, H. B. Cunningham, the 16-year-old Marlin purchased a 1966 Chevelle to race at the Nashville Speedway. Soon

Marlin's Chip Ganassi Racing crew changes tires and adds fuel during a race at Atlanta Motor Speedway in spring 2004.

after, in only his third start in a race car, Marlin relieved his father in a NASCAR Nextel Cup event at Nashville on July 17, 1976. He finished eighth. A year later, he joined his father for his first superspeedway race, running an ARCA (American Race Car Association) car at Talladega.

Marlin continued on the short tracks and won three consecutive track championships at the Nashville Speedway in 1980, 1981, and 1982. He campaigned the full Winston Cup schedule in 1983 and went on to win Rookie of

Former crew chief Lee McCall stands alongside Marlin during one of the more quiet moments at the race track.

Marlin's No. 40 Dodge is sleek and low to the road for better aerodynamics.

Marlin shares a moment with teammate Casey Mears, a rookie driver in 2004.

Marlin leads Jimmie Johnson (48), Brian Vickers (25), Greg Biffle (16), Jeremy Mayfield (19), and Ryan Newman (12) at speed.

After nearly 300 starts and nine second-place finishes, Marlin earned his first Winston Cup victory at the 1994 Daytona 500. He defended his Daytona 500 crown the following year, making him only the third driver in history to claim back-to-back Daytona 500 triumphs. Four more victories followed with McClure in 1995 and 1996: two at Talladega, one at Darlington, and a July win at Daytona.

After four winless seasons, Marlin rebounded with new team owner Ganassi in 2001, capturing two checkered flags and the third-place spot in the final points standings. The 2002 campaign started off well, with Marlin taking, and holding, the top spot in the point standings for 25 events on the schedule. He solidified his lead with victories at Las Vegas and Darlington in March, and by finishing in the Top 10 in eight of the first 10 races. A potentially serious neck injury sidelined him for the final seven events. Still, he remained optimistic.

Marlin returned in 2003 but went winless through the first 30 events. Further, no wins came in the first 23 events of 2004. Still, Marlin remains upbeat concerning his efforts and the efforts of his race team.

"We've had some problems along the way this season, but still, it's been good," Marlin says. "We've had some bad luck and we've hurt ourselves a little. We've just got to keep digging."

the Year honors driving for Roger Hamby.

Marlin struggled with various team owners until 1986, when he joined Billy Hagan for four full seasons. Two more seasons with Junior Johnson and one with Stavola Brothers Racing set the stage for his greatest successes, with Morgan-McClure Racing and later with Chip Ganassi.

MARK MARTIN

Mark Martin, driver of the Roush Racing Ford, doesn't usually come up with elaborate game plans. If he is out of contention for the win, a strong finish in the Top 5 is the next best thing. But Martin is also a realist and realizes just how hard winning NASCAR Nextel Cup events can be. The competition gets tougher with each passing season, and more drivers and teams have the money and talent to win races.

Still, Martin finds a way to meet that challenge, as he has finished in the Top-5 point standings on 10 occasions and the Top 10 in points 13 times.

Even when he was racing as a teenager back in the early 1970s, Martin was no different. He battled veteran drivers such as Bobby Allison, Dick Trickle, and Jim Sauter for American Speed Association (ASA) victories. Long before he was of legal age, Martin mastered the tracks of the Midwest better than some with twice the experience. He racked up hundreds of wins in addition to four ASA championships.

Born:	January 9, 1959, Batesville, Arkansas
Height:	5-6
Weight:	135 lbs

Sponsor	**Pfizer/Viagra**
Make	**Ford**
Crew Chief	**Pat Tryson**
Team	**Jack Roush**

Mark Martin holds his trophy high at the Dover International Speedway in June 2004.

Martin took his winning ways to the Winston Cup arena in 1981, using a couple of his own Buick Regals. He scored two pole positions that year, one Top 5, and one Top 10. The strong start grabbed the attention of more than one team owner, but Martin again fielded his own team for the full schedule in 1982. He came up short to Geoff Bodine in the Rookie of the Year race, and fell short to the bank for the many

NASCAR NEXTEL Cup Career Statistics

YEAR	RACES	WINS	TOP 5S	TOP 10S	POLES	TOTAL POINTS	FINAL STANDING	WINNINGS
1981	5	0	1	2	2	615	42nd	$13,950
1982	30	0	2	8	0	3,181	14th	$126,655
1983	16	0	1	3	0	1,621	30th	$99,655
1986	5	0	0	0	0	488	48th	$20,515
1987	1	0	0	0	0	46	---	$3,550
1988	29	0	3	10	1	3,142	15th	$223,630
1989	29	1	14	18	6	4,053	3rd	$1,019,250
1990	29	3	16	23	3	4,404	2nd	$1,302,958
1991	29	1	14	17	5	3,914	6th	$1,039,991
1992	29	2	10	17	1	3,887	6th	$1,000,571
1993	30	5	12	19	5	4,150	3rd	$1,657,622
1994	31	2	15	20	1	4,250	2nd	$1,628,906
1995	31	4	13	22	4	4,320	4th	$1,893,519
1996	31	0	14	23	4	4,278	5th	$1,887,396
1997	32	4	16	24	3	4,681	3rd	$2,532,484
1998	33	7	22	26	3	4,964	2nf	$4,309,006
1999	34	2	19	26	1	4,943	3rd	$3,509,744
2000	34	1	13	20	0	4,410	8th	$3,098,874
2001	36	0	3	15	2	4,095	12th	$3,797,006
2002	36	1	12	22	0	4,762	2nd	$5,279,400
2003	36	0	5	10	0	3,769	17th	$4,048,847
2004	36	1	10	15	0	6,399	4th	$3,948,500
TOTALS	602	34	215	340	41	80,372		$42,442,069

Roush Racing's No. 6 Ford has had Mark Martin's name associated with it since he joined team owner Jack Roush in 1988. Here, he is seen racing at Martinsville (VA) Speedway.

dollars spent. His only chance to survive was as a hired gun for an owner hoping to make it big.

What followed was bittersweet. Team owner J. D. Stacy hired Martin in 1983 for what was to be a full schedule of racing. However, after only seven races, including a third-place finish at Darlington, Stacy fired Martin, a move that remains a mystery to some.

For the remainder of the 1983 season and over the next few years, Martin picked up rides wherever he could, first with D. K. Ulrich, then in five events with J. Gunderman in 1986, and one event for Roger Hamby in 1987. It was a tough existence. Then came the break of a lifetime.

Martin's crew gives him fresh left-side tires during one of the many pit stops they perform.

Martin leads Tony Stewart (20), Jeremy Mayfield (19), Greg Biffle (16), Ryan Newman (12), and Dale Jarrett in very close quarters for position.

Martin is often quiet while sitting idle at the race track.

Martin is definitely a fan favorite. Here he speeds past a packed grandstand of stock car racing fans.

Automotive engineer Jack Roush was forming a NASCAR Nextel Cup team and needed an experienced driver. Martin got word that a search was on, and he convinced Roush to hire him. Money was never a consideration. His only desire was to be back with an established team in Nextel Cup competition.

At the start of the 1988 season, Roush recognized Martin's burning desire to win and hired him over a long list of applicants. The first victory came on October 22, 1989, at North Carolina Motor Speedway in Rockingham. Since then, Martin and Roush have scored 17 more victories and 29 pole positions, and have established themselves as winners in the NASCAR Busch Series.

Although the wins have dwindled in recent years, the 34 career victories Martin has collected rank him 17th on the all-time win list. He's not quite ready to hang it up.

"I've always said that's why I race, because I love to be competitive," Martin says. "I love to run up front and to pass cars and to be in a position to win races, and we've done that several times this year, despite all of the rotten luck we've had."

JEREMY MAYFIELD

19

Owensboro, Kentucky, seems to be an unofficial racing capital of sorts, since several very successful NASCAR stars have come from Owensboro.

Jeremy Mayfield, driver of the Evernham Motorsports Dodge, joins a long list of drivers who hail from that southern town, including the three Green brothers (David, Mark, and Jeff) and the Waltrips (Michael and three-time champ Darrell). Whatever the reason, Mayfield certainly has the talent to make big things happen racing against his fellow Owensboro natives.

Like so many southern stock car drivers, Mayfield began his career as a go kart racer and eventually moved through the ranks of Street Stocks, Sportsman, and Late Models. Winning the 1987 Rookie of the Year award at Kentucky Motor Speedway brought Mayfield

Jeremy Mayfield put the No. 19 Evernham Motorsports Dodge in victory lane in 2004. His solid-red machine is known for its lime-green frontal tape and top number, distinguishing it from the No. 9 driven by teammate Kasey Kahne.

one step closer to his dream of driving and winning at the NASCAR Winston Cup level. He became a regular on the ARCA circuit in 1993 and had finishes good enough to earn him his second rookie honor.

Mayfield finally made his Winston Cup debut at Charlotte in October 1993, driving for team

Born:	May 27, 1969, Owensboro, Kentucky
Height:	6-0
Weight:	190 lbs

Sponsor	**Dodge Dealers**
Make	**Dodge**
Crew Chief	**Kenny Francis**
Team	**Ray Evernham**

Mayfield studies information given to him concerning his car's handling characteristics.

owner Earl Sadler. Sadler had fielded cars for several notable up-and-coming drivers—including the late Davey Allison—so Mayfield appeared to be on the right path. He wheeled Sadler cars for four races in 1994, and T. W. Taylor also brought Mayfield on for four events that year. Then NASCAR legend Cale Yarborough called and asked for Mayfield's services. Many predicted it would be a prosperous marriage, but after 12 races in 1994 and a full season in 1995, the wins simply didn't come.

Late in the season in 1996, owners Yarborough and Michael Kranefuss swapped

NASCAR NEXTEL Cup Career Statistics

YEAR	RACES	WINS	TOP 5S	TOP 10S	POLES	TOTAL POINTS	FINAL STANDING	WINNINGS
1993	1	0	0	0	0	76	---	$4,830
1994	20	0	0	0	0	1,673	37th	$226,265
1995	27	0	0	1	0	2,637	31st	$436,805
1996	30	0	2	2	1	2,721	26th	$592,853
1997	32	0	3	8	0	3,547	13th	$1,067,203
1998	33	1	12	16	1	4,157	7th	$2,332,034
1999	34	0	5	12	0	3,743	11th	$2,125,227
2000	32	2	6	12	4	3,307	24th	$2,169,251
2001	28	0	5	7	0	2,651	35th	$2,682,603
2002	36	0	2	4	0	3,309	26th	$2,494,580
2003	36	0	4	12	1	3,736	19th	$2,962,228
2004	36	1	5	13	2	6,000	10th	$3,892,570
TOTALS	345	4	44	87	9	27,577		$20,986,449

Mayfield has made No. 19 prominent among front-runners in 2004. Here he is shown doing what he does best—making it go fast.

drivers. Mayfield went to work for Kranefuss, while John Andretti went over to Yarborough's team. (Andretti won the 400-mile event at Daytona for Yarborough in 1997.)

After Kranefuss joined with racing legend Roger Penske, Mayfield had the best ride of his career. He scored wins at Pocono, Pennsylvania, in 1998 and 2000, as well as a win at California in 2000. In addition, there were pole positions at Darlington, Dover, Rockingham, Talladega, and Texas.

Despite the two wins, not all was well in 2000, as things slowly unraveled for the

Mayfield, sporting his trademark flattop haircut, is a favorite among the fans.

The Evernham Motorsports Dodge that Mayfield drives is easy to pick out on the race track, due in part to its solid-red paint scheme.

Mayfield can often be seen as intense (left) or can be seen relaxing behind a pair of sunglasses while waiting for race action to begin.

Penske-Mayfield partnership. When Mayfield's car was found to be too low after the California win, it seemed to mark the beginning of the end. Even though Mayfield had nothing to do with the height of the car, there was discord within the team. Finally, after an additive was put in his gas tank by a crew member just before Mayfield's pole position run at Talladega, the end was all but written.

Apparently, both owner and driver wanted and needed a change after the tumultuous 2000 campaign. Mayfield finally got his wish the day after the inaugural event at Kansas Speedway in September 2001, when Penske

Racing released Mayfield from his contract. From that day until the start of Speedweek 2002, which kicked off the new season, Mayfield sat on the sidelines waiting for a new ride. Finally, Evernham Motorsports came along, and a new relationship was formed.

Mayfield had not won a race with Evernham through the first 30 events of 2003 and received a great deal of criticism for not finding victory lane with such a strong organization. A win was equally hard to find in 2004, but at least Mayfield kept his name in the mix as one who could sneak into the Top-10 Chase for the Championship standings.

"To start with, it looked like it was going to be OK, and then we had a few bad races, and then all of a sudden we kept staying focused on what we've had to do," Mayfield says. "We've been racing every week just like there's no pressure, nothing to worry about, and just doing the best we can as a race team and racking up all the points we can.

"We've really got the momentum going, and we're communicating well, and everything's going great and that's what me and Kenny Francis, my crew chief, you know, things just keep getting better and better every week."

JAMIE McMURRAY

42

Of all the drivers who compete in NASCAR Nextel Cup competition, it seemed as though Jamie McMurray, driver of the Chip Ganassi Racing Dodge, was the hottest commodity of 2004. His name surfaced at both Joe Gibbs Racing as well as Penske Racing as a driver they would love to have behind the controls of their respective Chevrolets and Dodges.

And there's good reason why. McMurray joined the NASCAR Nextel Cup circuit in late 2002 and proved that Cinderella finishes can unfold and dreams really do come true. Of the millions of fans and the close-knit NASCAR fraternity witnessing the conclusion of the 500-mile event at Lowe's Motor Speedway on October 13, McMurray was probably the most surprised of them all at the outcome.

To set the stage, veteran driver Sterling Marlin was injured in a crash at Kansas on September 29 and couldn't compete for the

Born:	June 3, 1976, Joplin, Missouri
Height:	5-9
Weight:	150 lbs

Sponsor	**Havoline**
Make	**Dodge**
Crew Chief	**Donnie Wingo**
Team	**Chip Ganassi**

McMurray drives a car with a paint scheme that the late Davey Allison made famous. McMurray sports the number *42*, while Allison's number was *28*.

McMurray seems to be enjoying his place in the sun as he's dressed in his black-and-red Havoline team colors.

NASCAR NEXTEL Cup Career Statistics

YEAR	RACES	WINS	TOP 5S	TOP 10S	POLES	TOTAL POINTS	FINAL STANDING	WINNINGS
2003	36	0	5	13	1	3,965	13th	$2,699,969
2004	36	0	9	23	0	4,597	11th	$3,676,310
TOTALS	72	0	14	36	1	8,562		$6,376,279

rest of the season, after leading the point standings for 25 consecutive weeks. Team owner Chip Ganassi had had his eye on McMurray as a possible third-team driver in 2003 but had not yet presented him with a contract. McMurray started his tenure

McMurray comes to a stop on pit road while his crew "rebuilds" his car with new tires and a full tank of fuel.

with the Mooresville, North Carolina–based team at Talladega, Alabama, October 6 with a 26th-place finish. Most everyone thought this was going to be another story of a "NASCAR Busch Series gets a Winston Cup ride" only to need months to prove himself. Nothing could have been further from the truth.

McMurray thanked Ganassi for having confidence in him by rolling into victory lane after a long, hard-fought battle with veteran Bobby Labonte in the 500-mile event at Charlotte. He became the fifth driver to win in just his sec-

McMurray waits patiently inside his Chip Ganassi-owned Dodge. He is one of stock car racing's newest stars.

McMurray proves he is a good listener, as he stops to receive advice from his crew or fellow drivers.

ond outing and the first in NASCAR's modern era (dating back to 1972).

He is quickly rising to the top as a future superstar with a great deal of talent. Add flair and personality, and one can see why he has become a public-relations dream.

McMurray looks to be staying right where he is.

"We are excited about having Jamie as part of the team into the future," Ganassi says. "With the way the No. 42 Texaco/Havoline team has been running up front, we are in a position to start winning races soon."

McMurray makes a pit stop at Lowe's Motor Speedway while his crew gives him fresh right-side tires.

CASEY MEARS

41

Auto racing enthusiasts may notice that the name of Casey Mears, driver of the Chip Ganassi Racing Dodge, seems quite familiar. He is the nephew of Rick Mears, a four-time winner of the Indianapolis 500. He is also the son of two-time Indianapolis 500 starter and off-road legend Roger Mears.

The younger Mears stuck with the family's tradition by winning his first feature event at Masa Marin in 1994 at the mere age of 16.

From there, young Casey put together further impressive numbers.

He won the 1995 Jim Russell USAC Triple Crown championship at age 17 and followed that with three races of off-road competition in the SuperLites in 1996. In 1999, he finished second in the Indy Lights Series and became only the fourth driver in series history to complete every lap.

By 2000, the speeds were getting quite a bit higher. Mears successfully completed his

Born:	March 12, 1978, Bakersfield, California
Height:	5-8
Weight:	158 lbs

Sponsor	**Target**
Make	**Dodge**
Crew Chief	**Jimmy Elledge**
Team	**Chip Ganassi**

Casey Mears takes his No. 41 Ganassi Racing Dodge to its limits in his first year of competition. His Dodge carries one of the more unique paint schemes.

Casey Mears, the nephew of Indy car great Rick Mears, is trying to make his mark as a stock car driver. Here, he peaks out from behind the shield of his helmet.

NASCAR NEXTEL Cup Career Statistics

YEAR	RACES	WINS	TOP 5S	TOP 10S	POLES	TOTAL POINTS	FINAL STANDING	WINNINGS
2003	36	0	0	0	0	2,638	35th	$2,639,178
2004	36	0	1	9	2	3,690	22nd	$3,250,320
TOTALS	72	0	1	9	2	6,328		$5,889,498

rookie test for the Indianapolis 500 in 2000. That same year, he finished third in the Indy Lights Series, scoring his first win at the Grand Prix of Houston.

By then, stock cars had come into the picture. Mears finished ninth in an ARCA event in 2001, and by the following year had a full-time ride in the NASCAR Busch Series, where he finished two Top 10s in 34 starts. In December

Mears has sported various colors on his car in 2004. Here is he shown making a pit stop in his green-and-white paint scheme.

of that year, he announced he would drive for team owner Chip Ganassi in NASCAR's highest division for the entire 2003 season.

No wins came to the young star, but he did manage to gain quite a bit of experience racing against the likes of fellow teammates Jamie McMurray and Sterling Marlin, as well as a virtual Who's Who of NASCAR stars.

In 2004, Mears really began showing his muscle. So why is he now running so well among the leaders?

"I think it's just experience with everybody," Mears says. "It's the experience

Mears had adapted well to the pressures of stock car racing and has posted some impressive finishes. He has shown promise as a rookie.

Mears sits amid roll bars and other various pieces of equipment that keep him safe. Here, he sits in the garage area ready to be given the signal for practice.

with [crew chief] Jimmy [Elledge] and I working together. We've found what I like in the cars, and we're still learning that. We're nowhere near where we were last year as far as setups go. We've kinda narrowed it down to what I like. The biggest thing I've found we've improved is our Happy Hour and our practice sessions. When we end Happy Hour now, I know if I've got a good car or a bad car. Now, I know by feel. I've had experience at some of these tracks, and I know what it felt like if my car was good."

Mears is all smiles, something that comes easily when driving for a top-flight team.

JOE NEMECHECK

25

For Joe Nemechek, the rule has always been that if it goes fast, it's ready to race. From the time Joe and his late brother, John, were old enough to reach the pedals on their bicycles, they dreamed of becoming stars in NASCAR. Sadly, at the young age of 27, John Nemechek lost his life in an accident during a NASCAR Craftsman Truck Series event in March 1997.

From an early age, Joe Nemechek has had the word *champion* associated with his name. He began racing motocross at age 13, winning more than 300 trophies in six years, before entering the realm of short-track events in his native Florida in 1987.

Never one to do anything halfway, Nemechek won Rookie of the Year honors and championships in three straight years: the Southeastern Mini Stock Series in 1987, the U.S.A.R. Series in 1988, and the All-Pro Series in 1989. He went on to take the NASCAR Busch Series championship in 1992 before officially joining the NASCAR Winston Cup

Nemechek proudly displays the U.S. Army colors on his Nelson Bowers–owned Chevrolet. He carried those colors to victory at Kansas in October 2004.

ranks in 1993. To date, he is a two-time winner in Winston Cup and has collected nearly $10 million in earnings.

In 2002, Nemechek joined Hendrick Motorsports, replacing Jerry Nadeau. The result late in the season showed promising results with crew chief Peter Sospenzo.

In 2003, Nemechek and Sospenzo pulled off a strong victory at Richmond, Virginia, on May 3.

Born: September 26, 1963, Lakeland, Florida
Height: 5-9
Weight: 185 lbs

Sponsor	**US Army**
Make	**Chevrolet**
Crew Chief	**Ryan Pemberton**
Team	**Nelson Bowers**

Even so, the 10-year veteran lost his ride with Hendrick to make way for the younger NASCAR Busch Series standout Brian Vickers. It was simply a matter of business, as Vickers brought sponsorship to a team losing sponsorship dollars.

In late 2003, Nemechek landed a ride with MB2 Motorsports and has now signed a long-term agreement with the team. The team suffered through a series of finishes that could be considered less than desirable, some of which were not of the team's making. Nemechek feels good about things around the corner.

"This is a strong race team. Stronger than some people might think," Nemechek says. "I think we're on the verge of winning some races. We've got all the pieces in place to get it done."

NASCAR NEXTEL Cup Career Statistics

YEAR	RACES	WINS	TOP 5S	TOP 10S	POLES	TOTAL POINTS	FINAL STANDING	WINNINGS
1993	5	0	0	0	0	389	44th	$56,580
1994	29	0	1	3	0	2,673	27th	$389,565
1995	29	0	1	4	0	2,742	28th	$428,925
1996	29	0	0	2	0	2,391	34th	$666,247
1997	30	0	0	3	2	2,754	28th	$732,194
1998	32	0	1	4	0	2,897	26th	$1,343,991
1999	34	1	1	3	3	2,956	30th	$1,634,946
2000	34	0	3	9	1	3,534	15th	$2,105,042
2001	31	1	1	4	0	2,994	28th	$2,510,723
2002	33	0	3	3	0	2,682	34th	$2,453,020
2003	36	1	2	6	0	3,426	25th	$2,560,484
2004	36	1	3	9	2	3,878	19th	$3,872,410
TOTALS	358	4	16	50	8	33,316		$18,754,127

Nemechek has been a fixture on the circuit for the past decade and has gone to victory lane on five occasions.

RYAN NEWMAN

12

Ryan Newman, driver of the Penske Racing Dodge, has had a reputation for winning races through engineering practices. After all, he's a graduate of Purdue University with a degree in engineering. But his real claim to fame, at least among team owners, is his ability to wrestle an open-wheel sprint car around a dirt short track in the Midwest. While growing up, Newman won countless races there while honing his racing skills.

Ever since Rick Hendrick discovered Jeff Gordon in the open-wheel sprint car ranks, other team owners have scoured the sprint grids for potential future champions. When team owners Roger Penske, Don Miller, and Rusty Wallace went out looking for new talent,

Born:	December 8, 1977, South Bend, Indiana
Height:	5-11
Weight:	207 lbs

Sponsor	**ALLTEL**
Make	**Ford**
Crew Chief	**Matt Borland**
Team	**Roger Penske**

Ryan Newman takes his No. 12 Penske Racing Dodge around one of many turns he has traveled during his career. The Purdue University graduate has used his engineering knowledge to help him win races.

Newman looks serious as he stands by his pit box on pit road, possibly after falling out of an event.

they discovered Ryan Newman, a 24-year-old open-wheel star who is already in the Quarter Midget Hall of Fame.

Having been named to Penske's organization carried a huge amount of clout, as Penske is known in several forms of auto racing around the world for having the best equipment and talent that money can buy. Having the endorsement of Wallace, the 1989 NASCAR Winston Cup champion, made acceptance in the garage area a bit easier. From there, Newman would slowly gain their respect on and off the racetrack.

NASCAR NEXTEL Cup Career Statistics

YEAR	RACES	WINS	TOP 5S	TOP 10S	POLES	TOTAL POINTS	FINAL STANDING	WINNINGS
2000	1	0	0	0	0	40	---	$37,825
2001	7	0	2	2	1	652	49th	$465,276
2002	36	1	14	22	6	4593	6th	$4,373,830
2003	36	8	17	22	11	4711	6th	$4,827,377
2004	36	2	11	14	9	6,180	7th	$5,152,670
TOTALS	116	11	44	60	27	16,176		$14,856,978

Newman shows his excitement after winning an event at Michigan International Speedway in 2004. He is known for his burn-outs when he wins a race.

With his degree in vehicular structural engineering, Newman had some unique skills in setting up Winston Cup machines. He pulled off wins in ARCA competition at Pocono, Kentucky Speedway, and Charlotte. He was also victorious in all three USAC divisions: midgets, sprint cars, and the Silver Bullet Series.

Newman competed in both the Winston Cup and Busch Series in 2001, and his impact on the scene was almost immediate. In only his third career Winston Cup start, he scored a pole position in the 600-mile event at Charlotte. In seven starts that season, Newman kept his

Newman checks the radio connection on his helmet just before the start of an event. Being able to talk via two-way radio is vital in today's racing arena.

Newman (12) leads Jeff Burton (99) during an event in 2004.

Newman's Penske Racing Dodge is serviced in the last pit stall on pit road. It is often reserved for the pole position winner, an honor Newman has enjoyed many times during his brief career.

Newman's eyes show his eagerness to get strapped into his race car for the job at hand.

Penske Racing Ford up front on several occasions. He grabbed a fifth-place finish at Michigan in June, and topped that with a second-place running, behind Jeff Gordon, at Kansas Speedway's inaugural race in September.

In 2002, Newman won at Loudon, New Hampshire, and collected that elusive first NASCAR Winston Cup victory. Even though weather dictated NASCAR's decision to red-flag the event in its late stages, the win was still his. So many within the sport had predicted, without a doubt, that he would win Winston Cup events. Even more insiders predicted that he would continue to score victories each season and establish himself as a rising superstar. All

one has to do is look at his 2002 statistics of 14 Top 5s and 22 Top 10s to see that his rise to the top is moving quickly.

Those numbers also proved to be the foundation for winning 2002 Rookie of the Year honors. After a hard-fought battle with Jimmie Johnson, driver of the Hendrick Motorsports Chevrolet, Newman's smoothness behind the wheel of his race cars and behind the microphone during interviews proved he had the charisma to represent NASCAR well.

In 2003, Newman certainly showed the veteran drivers how to get the job done with eight wins and 11 pole positions. The 2004 season wasn't quite as glorious, with

only one win at Michigan through June, but it was still impressive.

"My degree helps me more with my communication skills. It's all about understanding the race car and being able to explain what's happening inside the car to the crew chief and the guys on the team," Newman says. "In turn, they understand that same language, whether it's terminology or through hand maneuvers, for me to be able to tell them how the car feels. We have to then adapt my thought process to their thought process and in turn make the correct adjustments to the car to make it better. It's what everyone calls chemistry. It's just a matter of it being engineering and chemistry at the same time."

KYLE PETTY

When your last name is Petty and your father is known as "The King" of stock car racing, your career is pretty much pre-ordained. Even before he ever drove a race car, Kyle Petty was being touted as a star of the future. He was the talk of racing circles at home and abroad.

Surely he would be a chip off the old block, they said.

As a child, Kyle saw stock car racing as nothing more than his father's profession. The cars in the nearby shop were shiny blue with painted numbers on their doors, set up to be turned left around short tracks and

Born:	June 2, 1960, Trinity, North Carolina
Height:	6-2
Weight:	195 lbs

Sponsor	**Georgia Pacific**
Make	**Dodge**
Crew Chief	**Bill Henderson**
Team	**Petty Enterprises**

NASCAR NEXTEL Cup Career Statistics

YEAR	RACES	WINS	TOP 5S	TOP 10S	POLES	TOTAL POINTS	FINAL STANDING	WINNINGS
1979	5	0	0	1	0	559	37th	$10,810
1980	15	0	0	6	0	1,690	28th	$36,350
1981	31	0	1	10	0	3,335	12th	$112,289
1982	29	0	2	4	0	3,024	15th	$120,730
1983	30	0	0	2	0	3,261	13th	$157,820
1984	30	0	1	6	0	3,159	16th	$324,555
1985	28	0	7	12	0	3,523	9th	$296,367
1986	29	1	4	14	0	3,537	10th	$403,242
1987	29	1	6	14	0	3,732	7th	$544,437
1988	29	0	2	8	0	3,296	13th	$377,092
1989	19	0	1	5	0	2,099	30th	$177,022
1990	29	1	2	14	2	3,501	11th	$746,326
1991	18	1	2	4	2	2,078	31st	$413,727
1992	29	2	9	17	3	3,945	5th	$1,107,063
1993	30	1	9	15	1	3,860	5th	$914,662
1994	31	0	2	7	0	3,339	15th	$806,332
1995	30	1	1	5	0	2,638	30th	$698,875
1996	28	0	0	2	0	2,696	27th	$689,041
1997	32	0	2	9	0	3,455	15th	$984,314
1998	33	0	0	2	0	2,675	30th	$1,287,731
1999	32	0	0	9	0	3,103	26th	$1,278,953
2000	19	0	0	1	0	1,441	41st	$894,911
2001	24	0	0	0	0	1,673	43rd	$1,008,919
2002	36	0	0	1	0	3,501	42nd	$1,995,820
2003	33	0	0	0	0	2,414	37th	$2,293,222
2004	35	0	0	0	0	2,811	33rd	$2,780,130
TOTALS	713	8	51	168	8	74,345		$20,400,740

Kyle Petty puts his No. 45 Petty Enterprises Dodge to the test. Petty is a driver for and the chief executive officer of the famed Petty operation.

superspeedways. He was surrounded by the sounds of air grinders hitting metal and engines screaming on the dynamometer.

Kyle at first resisted the seemingly predetermined path to the oval track during his adventurous and trouble-filled teenage years, but he eventually turned his energies toward his destiny. To become a Winston Cup racer was a tough but reasonable goal for any young driver. To meet the high expectations that come with bearing the Petty name, under the intense scrutiny of the press and public, was a much different story.

At the start of Speedweek in 1979, Petty came to Daytona International Speedway with a Dodge Magnum, a discarded Winston Cup machine his father had used with no success

Petty (45) leads Jimmy Spencer (4) and Rick Craven (32) as he and Spencer battle for position.

the year before. Although it had a heavy box-like design, the car was perfect for the younger Petty, who entered it in ARCA competition.

Miraculously, Kyle met the media expectations right off the bat. He won the ARCA 200 in his first outing on a closed course. For a brief time, he was the only undefeated stock car driver in America.

His career launched, a total of 169 races passed before Petty found victory lane in Winston Cup competition. It came in 1986, at the short track in Richmond, Virginia, with the Wood Brothers team. The win established him as the first third-generation driver to win a

Petty is one of the most liked individuals in any garage area around the circuit.

Petty's No. 45 machine proudly sports red, white, and blue colors.

Petty listens to his two-way radio during a qualifying session. His team also fields the No. 43 Petty Enterprises Dodge driven by Jeff Green.

Petty can often be seen sporting a large smile as he walks through the garage area.

Winston Cup race. His grandfather, Lee, won his first race in 1949, and his father, Richard, first stood on the top spot in 1960. Kyle notched another win in 1987 at the Coca-Cola 600, his first superspeedway triumph.

Six more wins followed with team owner Felix Sabates, but the Cuban transplant and the North Carolina country boy parted ways in 1996 after eight seasons together. They had become as close as father and son, but the results on the track didn't warrant another year together.

Petty elected to field his own cars in 1997 and 1998, meeting only limited success. In 1999, he reopened Petty Enterprises, partly to field cars for his son Adam in the Busch Series and, eventually, Winston Cup. That dream came to a tragic end when young Adam was killed in a single-car accident during a practice session at New Hampshire International Raceway on May 12, 2000.

With a heavy heart, Petty continues to operate the famed Petty Enterprises, partly because he knew his son would have wanted the organization to continue to flourish.

Petty, now with over 700-career starts, continues to race because it's family tradition. And when he's not racing, he's heavily dedicated to charity work.

"Racing is what we do. That's my life. That's what I've always done," Petty says. "That's what my grandfather and my father and Adam after me came along and did. It's a family business. This is what we do, and this is the core of what we do. I think we're blessed to be in this sport at a time when you can, as you mature and as you get a little bit older, use this vehicle to other means. We're able to use it as a platform to not only do what we love to do, which is drive race cars, but to maybe make a broader impact on other people's lives and maybe on society in some ways."

SCOTT RIGGS

10

Scott Riggs, driver of the Valvoline/MB2 Motorsports Chevrolet, entered his first season of NASCAR Nextel competition with two very strong NASCAR Busch Series seasons behind him. He finished sixth in the 2003 title race after posting two wins, 11 Top 5s and 17 Top 10s. The year before, he finished 10th in the season-long point standings and established himself as a contender for the title for the majority of the races on the circuit.

Riggs was one of the top Late Model Stock Car drivers in NASCAR's Mid-Atlantic Region.

He was a two-time champion of the Southern National Speedway in Kenley, North Carolina, where he amassed 60 victories.

Like so many rookies before him, the first season of NASCAR Nextel Cup competition presents its challenges, often translating into disappointment and heartache. Riggs best finish of the season came at Dover, Delaware, in June with a fifth-place finish on the lead lap.

Riggs cites the fact he is a NASCAR Nextel Cup driver as the highlight of his 2004 season.

Born:	January 1, 1971, Bahama, North Carolina
Height:	5-8
Weight:	180 lbs

Sponsor	**Valvoline**
Make	**Chevrolet**
Crew Chief	**Doug Randolph**
Team	**Valvoline/MB2 Motorsports**

Riggs makes a pit stop while running the full Nextel Cup schedule in hopes of winning rookie of the year honors.

Scott Riggs is a former NASCAR Busch Series competitor who brings his talents to Nextel Cup competition. Here is he shown driving the No. 10 Chevrolet owned by Nelson Bowers.

Being one of a very elite group of drivers can give great confidence to a young rising star.

"I can't tell you how excited I am just to be a part of NASCAR Nextel Cup competition," Riggs said at the beginning of the 2004 season. "There are so many great race-car drivers around the country and to have this opportunity is hard to describe. My job now is to go out and learn what I can and try to get as many good finishes as possible. There's a lot to learn, but the only way to get that education is with seat time. That means qualifying well and making all of the races. Our goal for this season is to perform the best we can and take one step at a time."

NASCAR NEXTEL Cup Career Statistics

YEAR	RACES	WINS	TOP 5S	TOP 10S	POLES	TOTAL POINTS	FINAL STANDING	WINNINGS
2004	35	0	1	2	0	3,090	29th	$3,443,350

RICKY RUDD

Even though Ricky Rudd, driver of the Wood Brothers Ford, may admit he's closer to retirement than he once was, he still having fun doing about the only thing he's ever done in his life. With the addition of friend and twice former crew chief Michael

Born: September 12, 1956, Chesapeake, Virginia

Height: 5-8

Weight: 160 lbs

Sponsor	**Motorcraft**
Make	**Ford**
Crew Chief	**Michael McSwain**
Team	**Len and Eddie Wood**

NASCAR NEXTEL Cup Career Statistics

YEAR	RACES	WINS	TOP 5S	TOP 10S	POLES	TOTAL POINTS	FINAL STANDING	WINNINGS
1975	4	0	0	1	0	431	53rd	$4,345
1976	4	0	0	1	0	407	56th	$7,525
1977	25	0	1	10	0	2,810	17th	$68,448
1978	13	0	0	4	0	1,264	32nd	$49,610
1979	28	0	4	17	0	3,642	9th	$146,302
1980	13	0	1	3	0	1,319	32nd	$50,500
1981	31	0	14	17	3	3,991	6th	$381,968
1982	30	0	6	13	2	3,542	9th	$201,130
1983	30	2	7	14	4	3,693	9th	$257,585
1984	30	1	7	16	4	3,918	7th	$476,602
1985	28	1	13	19	0	3,857	6th	$512,441
1986	29	2	11	17	1	3,823	5th	$671,548
1987	29	2	10	13	0	3,742	6th	$653,508
1988	29	1	6	11	2	3,547	11th	$410,954
1989	29	1	7	15	0	3,608	8th	$534,824
1990	29	1	8	15	2	3,601	7th	$573,650
1991	29	1	9	17	1	4,092	2nd	$1,093,765
1992	29	1	9	18	1	3,735	7th	$793,903
1993	30	1	9	14	0	3,644	10th	$752,562
1994	31	1	6	15	1	4,050	5th	$1,044,441
1995	31	1	10	16	2	3,734	9th	$1,337,703
1996	31	1	5	16	0	3,845	6th	$1,503,025
1997	32	2	6	11	0	3,330	17th	$1,975,981
1998	33	1	1	5	0	3,131	22nd	$1,602,895
1999	34	0	3	5	1	2,922	31st	$1,632,011
2000	34	0	12	19	2	4,575	5th	$2,974,970
2001	36	2	14	22	1	4,706	4th	$4,878,027
2002	36	1	8	12	1	4,323	10th	$4,009,380
2003	36	0	4	5	0	3,521	23rd	$3,106,614
2004	36	0	1	3	1	3,615	24th	$3,717,100
TOTALS	839	23	192	364	29	100,418		$35,423,317

Ricky Rudd, a longtime veteran of NASCAR Nextel Cup racing, wheels the No. 21 Wood Brothers Ford. The Wood family has been involved in the sport for over 50 years.

McSwaim, there may be more fun, and more wins, on the horizon.

Rudd's youthful face has been seen in victory lane at least once every season for 17 years, making him one of the most consistent drivers on the Nextel Cup circuit. Along with his wins have come many pole positions and more than $26 million in career earnings.

Rudd began racing motocross and go karts at a very early age but didn't drive a stock car until he first sat down in a Winston Cup ride in 1975 at age 18. He took four starts that year with Bill Champion, and one Top-10 finish foretold Rudd's potential. In 1976, he started four more events, this time in cars fielded by his father, Al Rudd Sr., and reeled off another Top-

Rudd brings his No. 21 machine to a stop to get service from his crew. For many years, the Wood Brothers were the fastest pit crew in NASCAR and took their talents to Indianapolis for the 500 in 1965. They won the race with driver Jimmy Clark.

Rudd sits behind the wheel of his Ford, set to compete for the win. Rudd has collected 23 wins since joining the circuit in 1975.

10 finish—a hint of the consistency that would mark his lengthy career. With his family-owned team, Rudd tackled the majority of the schedule in 1977, competing in 25 events, and earned Rookie of the Year honors after finishing 17th in the point standings that season.

Rudd came back to start in 13 races in 1978, garnering results sufficient to land a ride with longtime team owner Junie Donlavey for the full schedule in 1979. He scored two third-place finishes and two fifths in 1979, earning him nearly $150,000. Overall, it was a good learning season for Rudd.

Rudd rests while watching his crew work on his car.

With helmet on, Rudd is ready to take his No. 21 Ford back on the racing surface. He has driven for some of the most prominent teams in history.

In 1980, back with the Rudd family operation for 13 events, Ricky found himself in a make-or-break situation. Money was running out fast, but one good race could get him noticed by the better-financed teams on the circuit, providing perhaps his only chance to remain an active driver. That October, Rudd entered the National 500 at Charlotte Motor Speedway in a year-old car and qualified on the outside front row. By race's end, Rudd was fourth, finishing behind legends Dale Earnhardt, Cale Yarborough, and Buddy Baker. As hoped, the impressive run caught the notice of several veteran team owners.

Rudd signed with DiGard Racing for the 1981 season, replacing Darrell Waltrip. Even though the results from the DiGard-Rudd union weren't overly impressive, there were definite signs of promise.

Rudd switched to the Richard Childress team in 1982, and his first Winston Cup victory came the following year at the Budweiser 400 in Riverside, California. Over the next few years, Rudd won six races driving for Bud Moore, two more with Kenny Bernstein, and captured four wins and a second-place finish in the 1991 Winston Cup point championship with Rick Hendrick.

Since then, he has scored more victories with his own team and with Robert Yates, a longtime friend he joined at the start of the 2000 season.

Since entering the NASCAR Nextel Cup circuit, Rudd's name has surfaced each season as a driver who is a constant threat for victory. With the Yates organization, Rudd had longtime members of the press believing that he would return to championship status. That may come this season with Rudd's current Wood Brothers operation, a team that's been around for over 50 years.

"I think we have to give it some time to let it work, but I'm pretty confident you're gonna see some improvements pretty quickly," Rudd says. "To sit here and say we're gonna win every race between here and the end of the year wouldn't be a true statement, but we're gonna take it a race at a time. The bad thing is it's happening in the middle of the season, but the good thing is it's happening to begin with because a guy like Fatback (McSwaim) isn't walking along unemployed very long. It's a rare opportunity for someone to pounce on it, so I have to commend the Wood Brothers for seeing that opportunity."

Rudd is all smiles as he listens to a story during a break in the action.

Rudd works his way around a turn while searching for a fast lap.

ELLIOTT SADLER

38

Elliott Sadler has enjoyed going fast since a rather young age. He began racing go karts at age seven. By the time he turned to stock cars at 18, he had compiled the same winning record as Richard Petty.

Before long, the urge to take his racing to a higher level brought Sadler to NASCAR's Busch Series. In 76 starts in the series, Sadler logged five victories and 12 Top 5s. His standout abilities caught the attention of brothers Len and Eddie Wood in 1999.

Wood Brothers Racing and the number they campaign are storied legends in NASCAR.

Sadler showed early in his Nextel Cup

Born:	April 30, 1975, Emporia, Virginia
Height:	6-2
Weight:	195 lbs

Sponsor	**M&M's**
Make	**Ford**
Crew Chief	**Todd Parrott**
Team	**Robert Yates**

Elliott Sadler, driver of the No. 38 Robert Yates Ford, drives one of the most colorful cars on the circuit. Many feel the colors mirror his personality.

Sadler, known for his distinctive Virginia accent, takes a break in the garage area while his crew services his car.

NASCAR NEXTEL Cup Career Statistics

YEAR	RACES	WINS	TOP 5S	TOP 10S	POLES	TOTAL POINTS	FINAL STANDING	WINNINGS
1998	2	0	0	0	0	128	---	$45,325
1999	34	0	0	1	0	3,191	24th	$1,589,221
2000	33	0	0	1	0	2,762	29th	$1,578,356
2001	36	1	2	2	0	3,471	20th	$2,683,225
2002	36	0	2	7	0	3,418	23rd	$3,390,690
2003	36	0	2	9	2	3,525	22nd	$3,660,174
2004	36	2	8	14	0	6,024	9th	$5,158,360
TOTALS	213	3	14	34	2	22,519		$18,105,351

career that he has the talent to follow in the footsteps of the great drivers of the past, such as Marvin Panch, Chris Turner, and David Pearson. He quickly repaid the Wood brothers' confidence in him with a win at Bristol Motor Speedway in April 2001.

For 2002, Sadler had no wins, two Top 5s, and seven Top 10s.

In 2003, Sadler joined Robert Yates Racing and enjoyed some promising finishes.

Sadler comes to a halt on pit road while his crew services his Ford during a pit stop. Usually during four-tire stops, the left-side tires are changed first.

Elliott Sadler (38) drops low and passes teammate Dale Jarrett (88) at Michigan International Speedway.

Victory lane, however, had eluded him through the first 30 events last season. In 2004, he recorded his second career win at Texas Motor Speedway on April 4.

"I definitely think I'm on the right path now. I feel like I'm with the right team," Sadler says. "I've got a great sponsor and great owners, and I want to be a part of this deal a long time. I would not give up anything that I've learned in the past over my 200 starts. I

Sadler shows his excitement after winning the Nextel Cup event at Texas Motor Speedway in the spring of 2004. Note the cowboy hat he wore in victory lane.

learned so much from Eddie and Len Wood about racing on and off the racetrack and about NASCAR. They helped me get to the position where I'm at today, so I wouldn't give up any of my learning experiences. Whether they were good or bad, they all make you a better person or shape you as a person. You've got to learn from your experiences on and off the track, and I feel like I've done that and I'm ready to move on."

Sadler smiles as he sits inside the Yates Ford, a car that is considered a powerhouse entry every week.

Sadler's brown eyes shine through the opening of his helmet as he sits strapped inside his Robert Yates Racing Ford.

JIMMY SPENCER

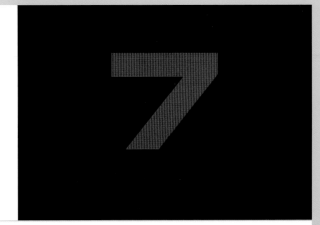

The native of Berwick, Pennsylvania, knows nothing but pushing the throttle to the floor and cranking the wheel hard left. In 1986 and 1987, Spencer showed he was serious about winning when he collected back-to-back Winston modified championships. He progressed the next season into the NASCAR Busch Series, and he continues to compete in that series along with his NEXTEL Cup efforts. In his first Winston Cup experience, Spencer ran 17 races in 1989 for legend-turned-owner Buddy Baker. There, too, Spencer showed great promise but just couldn't break into the winner's circle. Team owners Rod Osterlund and Travis Carter also enjoyed good finishes with Spencer in 1990 and 1991, respectively.

Because of Spencer's strong efforts in the series, another legendary former driver, Bobby Allison, invited him to join his team for the Winston Cup Series in 1992. Over a two-year period, Spencer had 13 Top-10 finishes in Allison's Fords.

At the start of the 1994 Winston Cup season, Spencer immediately showed his strength at the Daytona 500, and then went on to win the Pepsi 400 there in July and the DieHard 500 at Talladega three weeks later, notching victories at the two foremost restrictor-plate tracks.

Spencer elected to return to the cars fielded by Travis Carter in 1995, but found little success. Still, the driver and team owner remained together until the end of the 2001 season.

For 2002, Spencer hooked up with Chip Ganassi and Felix Sabates, driving Dodges for the first time in his career. Spencer could only muster two Top 5s and six Top 10s and was

Born: February 15, 1957, Berwick, Pennsylvania

Height: 6-0

Weight: 230 lbs

Sponsor	**Lucus Oil**
Make	**Chevrolet**
Crew Chief	**Tim Brewer**
Team	**Larry McClure**

released from the team at the end of the season. From there, Spencer elected to join Jim Smith in 2003 and enjoyed some strong runs. Still, the final statistics didn't reflect the team's true potential. And when Smith closed his NASCAR Nextel Cup operation, Spencer elected to join longtime team owner McClure, an owner who has won the Daytona 500 three times with Sterling Marlin and former driver Ernie Irvan.

"The only thing I want to do is race," Spencer says. "Even though we don't have a longtime sponsor right now, we're still a solid race team. I think with a few breaks we can have some good finishes and land a long-term sponsor."

NASCAR NEXTEL Cup Career Statistics

YEAR	RACES	WINS	TOP 5S	TOP 10S	POLES	TOTAL POINTS	FINAL STANDING	WINNINGS
1989	17	0	0	3	0	1,570	34th	$121,065
1990	26	0	0	2	0	2,579	24th	$219,775
1991	29	0	1	6	0	2,790	25th	$283,620
1992	12	0	3	3	0	1,284	33rd	$186,085
1993	30	0	5	10	0	3,496	12th	$686,026
1994	29	2	3	4	1	2,613	29th	$479,235
1995	29	0	0	4	0	2,809	26th	$507,210
1996	31	0	2	9	0	3,476	15th	$1,090,876
1997	32	0	1	4	0	3,079	20th	$1,073,779
1998	31	0	3	8	0	3,464	14th	$1,741,012
1999	34	0	2	4	0	3,312	20th	$1,752,299
2000	34	0	2	5	0	3,188	22nd	$1,936,762
2001	36	0	3	8	2	3,782	16th	$2,669,638
2002	34	0	2	6	0	3,187	27th	$2,136,790
2003	35	0	1	4	0	3,147	29th	$2,565,803
2004	26	0	0	0	0	1,969	35th	$1,985,120
TOTALS	475	2	28	80	3	45,745		$19,435,095

Jimmy Spencer on the track in his No.4 Chevy during the 2004 Nextel Cup season.

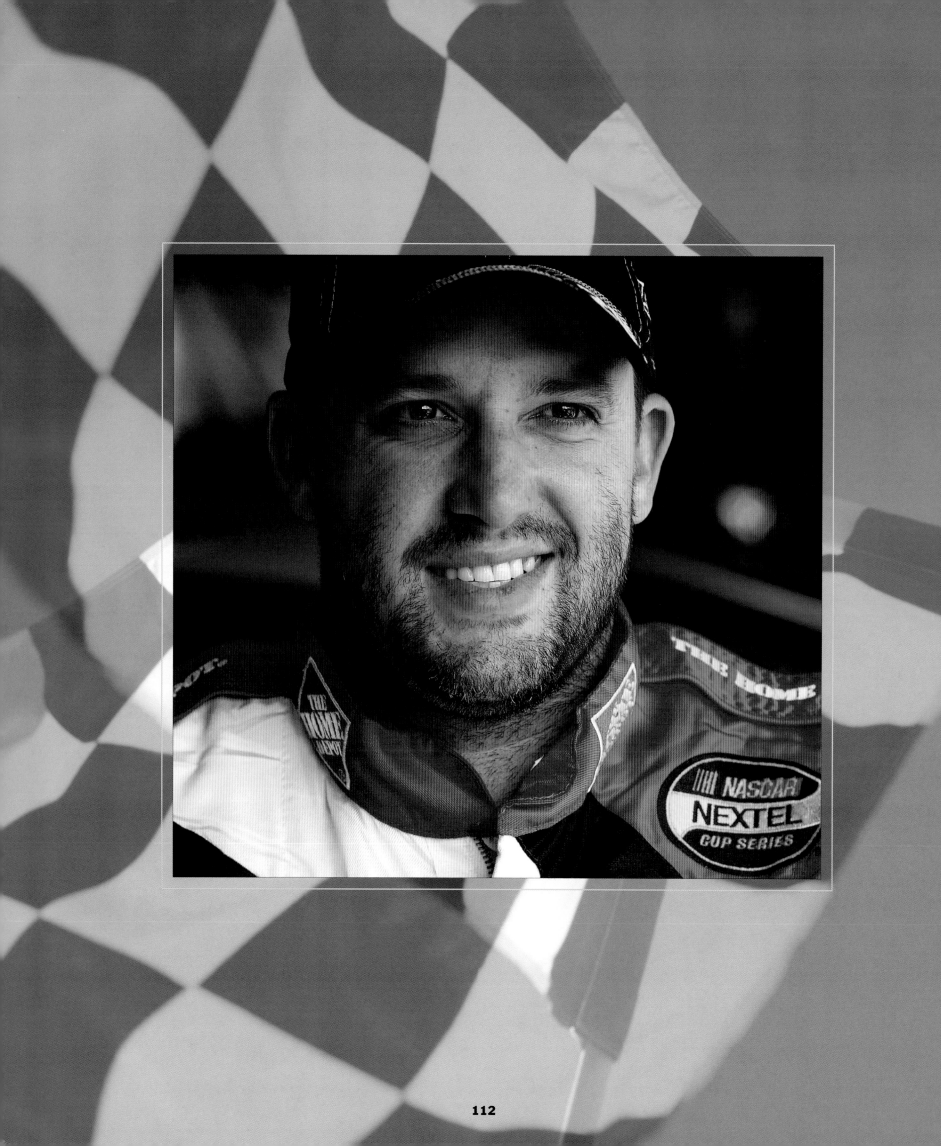

TONY STEWART

20

When Tony Stewart arrived in the NASCAR Winston Cup arena to drive Pontiacs for team owner Joe Gibbs, most everyone billed him as a likely instant winner. The Indiana native had already spent many years winning races in the open-wheel sprint car ranks as well as in the most elite of open-wheel arenas, the Indianapolis 500. With such tremendous talent established so early on, the gates of victory lane would most certainly not be padlocked long while he was around.

Stewart exceeded expectations and began his Winston Cup portfolio by breaking the record for wins by a rookie and winning the 1999 NASCAR Winston Cup Rookie of the Year.

Born:	May 20, 1971, Rushville, Indiana
Height:	5-9
Weight:	170 lbs

Sponsor	**Home Depot**
Make	**Chevrolet**
Crew Chief	**Greg Zipadelli**
Team	**Joe Gibbs**

Stewart sits contemplating his strategy just prior to race time.

Tony Stewart wheels his orange-and-black Joe Gibbs Racing Chevrolet at speed during one of his many events in 2004.

His first career victory came in his 25th start, at Richmond International Raceway in Virginia. By season's end, Stewart and his team were clicking well enough to win back-to-back races at Phoenix, Arizona, and Homestead, Florida.

Perhaps Stewart's most impressive accomplishment of 1999 was racing in both the Coca-Cola World 600 at Charlotte and the Indianapolis 500 on the same day.

After an exhaustive 1,100 miles of high-speed magic, he finished fourth in the 600 at Charlotte Motor Speedway and ninth in the 500 at Indianapolis Motor Speedway.

In 2000, many looked to Stewart to pull off the rare accomplishment of winning a Winston Cup championship the very next year after capturing rookie honors. Unfortunately, Stewart got

NASCAR NEXTEL Cup Career Statistics

YEAR	RACES	WINS	TOP 5S	TOP 10S	POLES	TOTAL POINTS	FINAL STANDING	WINNINGS
1999	34	3	12	21	2	4,774	4th	$3,190,149
2000	34	6	12	23	2	4,570	6th	$3,642,348
2001	36	3	15	22	0	4,763	2nd	$4,941,463
2002	36	3	15	21	4	4,800	1st	$4,695,150
2003	36	2	12	18	1	4,549	7th	$5,227,503
2004	36	2	10	19	0	6,326	6th	$6,221,710
TOTALS	212	19	76	124	9	29,782		$27,918,323

Stewart walks alongside his No. 20 Gibbs Racing Pontiac along with his crew as they move the car back to the garage area after qualifying.

Stewart hugs the frontstretch wall as he puts his Chevrolet to the test in a 2004 race.

off to a slow start in his sophomore season, ultimately finishing a respectable sixth in points, while teammate Bobby Labonte captured his first Winston Cup championship.

The next year, Tony Stewart enjoyed his best season to date. He started 2001 off with a victory in the Bud Shoot-Out, a special non-points event for pole-position winners. In June, he was a winner on the road course at Sears Point, California. He followed that performance with another victory at Richmond and also pulled off a win at the demanding high-banked short track of Bristol Motor Speedway. In the end, he finished second to Jeff Gordon in the overall championship hunt after coming on strong at the end when others suffered mechanical failures.

For the second time in his career, Stewart attempted the Charlotte–Indy double duty in 2001. He again finished strong, coming in sixth in the 500 and third in the 600 at Charlotte. He elected not to do so in 2002, knowing the championship race needed his full attention.

Stewart (20) leads teammate Mike Bliss (80) and Ryan Newman (12) through a turn while battling for track position. Stewart enjoys all types of racing and also campaigns on the Sprint Car circuit when his schedule permits.

That year, Stewart was successful and put together his first career NASCAR Nextel Cup championship with three victories, 15 Top 5s, and 21 Top 10s in 36 starts.

For 2003, Stewart enjoyed a win at Pocono, Pennsylvania, and several races where he challenged for the win but settled for Top-5 finishes.

In 2004, Stewart suffered through a hot-and-cold season, winning races at both Chicago and Watkins Glen, New York, through the month of August. There's a reason why strings of race wins are rare and why championships are so hard to get.

"The competition level is so tight now," Stewart says. "At the beginning of the year, you used to be able to pick about five guys who you thought had a realistic shot at winning a championship. But now, you can pick anywhere from 10 to 12 guys who have a legitimate shot at the championship. If you have a good year and some luck goes your way, you can run for a championship."

Stewart sits inside his Gibbs Racing Chevrolet as he confers with crew chief Greg Zippadeli. The two are very close friends and have enjoyed a great deal of success together since coming into the sport in 1999.

BRIAN VICKERS

25

For Brian Vickers, driver of the Hendrick Motorsports Chevrolet, racing became his passion in 1994 when he began racing go karts in hopes of a championship or two down the road. He accomplished that feat three times, in 1995, 1996, and 1997. Along with his world karting championship, Vickers was a four-time North Carolina karting champion, traveling the state from his Thomasville home. Coincidentally, that was about the time the aspiring young driver met NASCAR Nextel Cup driver Terry Labonte—now a teammate at Hendrick Motorsports—who was a neighbor a short half-mile down the road. Labonte ended up offering Vickers a ride, but it wasn't in a race car—it was in the back seat of the Labonte's passenger car en route to junior high school.

Vickers continued in a variety of stock car racing divisions, enjoying success in virtually all of them. A family-operated NASCAR Busch Series operation ensued in 2000, and Vickers

Born:	October 24, 1983, Thomasville, North Carolina
Height:	5-9
Weight:	155 lbs

Sponsor	**GMAC**
Make	**Chevrolet**
Crew Chief	**Peter Sospenzo**
Team	**Rick Hendrick**

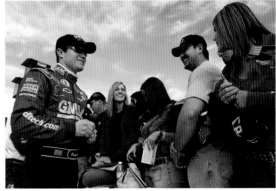

Vickers enjoys visiting with his fans at all of the Nextel Cup events. He is helping to bring a younger crowd to the sport of stock car racing.

eventually worked his way to entering 21 events the following season, posting one Top-10 finish. His efforts attracted the eye of then fellow driver Ricky Hendrick (son of team owner Rick Hendrick), and the two soon struck up a friendship. When Ricky Hendrick elected to retire as a driver after a hard crash, Vickers was tapped as his replacement, setting the wheels of opportunity in motion.

Vickers won the 2003 NASCAR Busch Series championship in Hendrick Chevrolets, winning three events.

Also that season, Vickers made his NASCAR Nextel Cup debut at Charlotte in October. He also made four more starts and qualified in the Top 5 in four of the five races. His best finish was 13th that year at Phoenix.

Brian Vickers, a rookie competitor in Nextel Cup competition in 2004, crosses the start/finish line in his Hendrick Motorsports Chevrolet.

NASCAR NEXTEL Cup Career Statistics

YEAR	RACES	WINS	TOP 5S	TOP 10S	POLES	TOTAL POINTS	FINAL STANDING	WINNINGS
2004	36	0	0	4	2	3,521	25th	$3,044,900

Vickers' crew swarms around his Hendrick Motorsports Chevrolet with tires and fuel in hand. Many four-tire stops are performed in just over 13 seconds.

Vickers drives No. 25, a number that the late Tim Richmond made famous for Hendrick Motorsports in 1986 and 1987. Here he is shown giving his car a full speed workout.

Vickers drives his black-and-blue No. 25 Hendrick Motorsports Chevrolet in hopes of winning rookie of the year honors. Many feel he has a very bright future as a Nextel Cup driver.

In 2004, Vickers best finishes have been an eighth at Richmond, a ninth at Michigan, and a ninth at Daytona.

"I've been offered a tremendous opportunity by Rick Hendrick and GMAC," Vickers says. "My goal when I joined Hendrick Motorsports was to be competitive each week and do everything possible to become better each race. We achieved those goals in the Busch Series, and I'm looking forward to similar results in the Cup Series.

"I don't pretend to know everything, and I realize I still have a lot to learn, but with the support of my family, friends, and the Hendrick organization, we can meet those expectations again."

With hood up on his car, Vickers sports a youthful look as he stands alongside his Hendrick Motorsports Chevrolet in the garage area.

RUSTY WALLACE

usty Wallace is undoubtedly one of the hottest stars in Winston Cup racing, having won at least one race every season since 1986.

When a bushy-haired Rusty Wallace brought a Roger Penske–owned Chevrolet to Atlanta Motor Speedway on March 16, 1980, the young Missourian wasn't supposed to have much of a chance since he was a rookie competing in his first Winston Cup event. He was leading with 29 laps to go when Dale Earnhardt passed him for the win. Wallace held on for second place, and his sensational debut was a sure sign of things to come.

Wallace won rookie honors in USAC competition in 1979 and was the 1983 ASA

Born:	August 14, 1956, Fenton, Missouri
Height:	6-0
Weight:	185 lbs

Sponsor	**Miller Lite**
Make	**Dodge**
Crew Chief	**Larry Carter**
Team	**Roger Penske**

NASCAR NEXTEL Cup Career Statistics

YEAR	RACES	WINS	TOP 5S	TOP 10S	POLES	TOTAL POINTS	FINAL STANDING	WINNINGS
1980	2	0	1	1	0	291	---	$22,760
1981	4	0	0	1	0	399	---	$12,895
1982	3	0	0	0	0	186	---	$7,655
1983	0	0	0	0	0	0	---	$1,100
1984	30	0	2	4	0	3,316	14th	$195,927
1985	28	0	2	8	0	2,867	19th	$233,670
1986	29	2	4	16	0	3,757	6th	$557,354
1987	29	2	9	16	1	3,818	5th	$690,652
1988	29	6	19	23	2	4,464	2nd	$1,411,567
1989	29	6	13	20	4	4,176	1st	$2,247,950
1990	29	2	9	16	2	3,676	6th	$954,129
1991	29	2	9	14	2	3,582	10th	$502,073
1992	29	1	5	12	1	3,556	13th	$657,925
1993	30	10	19	21	3	4,446	2nd	$1,702,154
1994	31	8	17	20	2	4,207	3rd	$1,914,072
1995	31	2	15	19	0	4,240	5th	$1,642,837
1996	31	5	8	18	0	3,717	7th	$1,665,315
1997	32	1	8	12	1	3,598	9th	$1,705,625
1998	33	1	15	21	4	4,501	4th	$2,667,889
1999	34	1	7	16	4	4,155	8th	$2,454,050
2000	34	4	12	20	9	4,544	7th	$3,621,468
2001	36	1	8	14	0	4,481	7th	$4,788,652
2002	36	0	7	17	1	4,574	7th	$4,090,050
2003	36	0	2	12	0	3,850	14th	$3,766,744
2004	36	1	3	11	0	3,960	16th	$4,447,300
TOTALS	670	55	194	332	36	84,461		$41,961,813

Rusty Wallace in the Miller Lite car during his 24th year of racing.

champion. In his first full season in NASCAR Winston Cup racing, Wallace became the 1984 Rookie of the Year.

Over a 17-year period, Wallace has collected 54 NASCAR Nextel Cup victories, 36 of them with Penske's organization. Now, all Wallace wants is more wins and at least one more championship before he turns his attention to other business ventures. The 2005 NASCAR Nextel Cup season will be his last as a driver.

"There's life after racing, even though I love racing," Wallace says. "But I'm positioning myself to step down one of these days, and when I do, it will be a real fluid movement.

"One of my goals before I retire is to win the Daytona 500. It's a race I've been close to many times but haven't won."

MICHAEL WALTRIP

15

Michael Waltrip is quick to tell you that stock cars aren't his only racing passion. The Owensboro, Kentucky, native has entered both the Boston Marathon and the Tampa Marathon. But it's in the NASCAR arena where his greatest talents lie, and like his teammate Kenny Wallace, Waltrip certainly knows how to hold court in any garage area.

The younger brother of three-time Winston Cup champion Darrell Waltrip, Michael is probably best known for his victory in the 2001 Daytona 500, in the 462nd start of a career dating back to 1985. The victory will forever be overshadowed by the death of Dale Earnhardt on the final lap. Coincidentally, Waltrip was driving a Chevrolet owned by Earnhardt. He was in the lead, two positions ahead of the legend, when the fatal crash occurred.

Waltrip returned to Daytona in July of that year and finished second to DEI teammate Dale Earnhardt Jr. in the 400-mile event. Waltrip now has over 500 starts in a career that also includes 21 Top 5s, 85 Top 10s, and two pole positions. Waltrip captured a second career victory in 2002, and once again the trophy was earned at the famous Daytona International Speedway. Waltrip's win in the

Born:	April 30, 1963, Owensboro, Kentucky	
Height:	6-5	
Weight:	210 lbs	

Sponsor	**NAPA**
Make	**Chevrolet**
Crew Chief	**Slugger Labbe**
Team	**DEI**

Michael Waltrip seems content as he sports his sponsorship colors for his fans. Waltrip has been racing in Nextel Cup competition since 1985.

Pepsi 400 that July supplied him with the encouragement he needed for continued success with DEI.

In 2003, Waltrip scored his second career Daytona 500 in a rain-shortened event. He

NASCAR NEXTEL Cup Career Statistics

YEAR	RACES	WINS	TOP 5S	TOP 10S	POLES	TOTAL POINTS	FINAL STANDING	WINNINGS
1985	5	0	0	0	0	395	49th	$9,540
1986	28	0	0	0	0	2,853	19th	$108,767
1987	29	0	0	1	0	2,840	20th	$205,370
1988	29	0	1	3	0	2,949	18th	$240,400
1989	29	0	0	5	0	3,067	18th	$249,233
1990	29	0	5	10	0	3,251	16th	$395,507
1991	29	0	4	12	2	3,254	15th	$440,812
1992	29	0	1	2	0	2,825	23rd	$410,545
1993	30	0	0	5	0	3,291	17th	$529,923
1994	31	0	2	10	0	3,512	12th	$706,426
1995	31	0	2	8	0	3,601	12th	$898,338
1996	31	0	1	11	0	3,535	14th	$1,182,811
1997	32	0	0	6	0	3,173	18th	$1,138,599
1998	32	0	0	5	0	3,340	17th	$1,508,680
1999	34	0	1	3	0	2,974	29th	$1,701,160
2000	34	0	1	1	0	2,792	27th	$1,689,421
2001	36	1	3	3	0	3,159	24th	$3,411,644
2002	36	1	4	10	0	3,985	14th	$2,829,180
2003	36	2	8	11	0	3,934	15th	$4,463,485
2004	36	0	2	9	0	3,878	20th	$4,245,690
TOTALS	606	4	35	115	2	62,608		$26,365,531

Waltrip (15) leads Dale Jarrett (88), Ken Schrader (49), Mark Martin (6), and Jeff Gordon (24) in hopes of securing a win.

followed that win by taking the checkered flag at Talladega Superspeedway in October to help the DEI cars dominate those two tracks.

In 2004, Waltrip fell on a winless streak through 23 events and was well out of position to enter the final 10 events with a shot at the championship. Still, he considered it to be a good season.

Waltrip, younger brother of three-time champion Darrell Waltrip, shows a determined look as he stands in the garage area.

Since 2001, Waltrip has driven the dark-blue-and-yellow colors of the No. 15 Chevrolet fielded by Dale Earnhardt, Inc. Waltrip is always a favorite among drivers and fans.

"We started the season off really well, but we fell into a slump and haven't full come out of it," Waltrip says. "We're working on that week to week. We have to get back to consistent wins and Top-5 finishes. I still feel the 2004 season has had its positives and high points."

Waltrip sits with helmet tight, staring into the distance. He has proven he's best on superspeedways like Daytona and Talladega.

SCOTT WIMMER

22

Even though relatively new to the world of NASCAR Nextel Cup racing, Scott Wimmer, driver of the Bill Davis Racing Dodge, has certainly shown promise since joining the circuit as a rookie at the beginning of the 2004 season.

Wimmer ran three full seasons in the NASCAR Busch Series with his best championship finish a third in 2002. He won four races in that division in 2002 at Dover, Delaware; Memphis, Tennessee; Phoenix, Arizona; and Homestead, Florida. The year

Born:	January 26, 1976, Wausau, Wisconsin
Height:	6-0
Weight:	180 lbs

Sponsor	**CAT**
Make	**Dodge**
Crew Chief	**Frank Stoddard**
Team	**Bill Davis Racing**

before, he finished 11th in the NASCAR Busch Series championship and was runner up to Greg Biffle for Rookie of the Year honors.

In 2000, Wimmer logged one NASCAR Nextel Cup star, finishing 22nd at Atlanta in his first start. He logged three starts in 2002 with a 19th at Phoenix, his best of the season.

When Ward Burton elected to end his driving relationship with David in 2003, Wimmer was tapped to take the ride with four races remaining in the season. All the while, he continued running the Busch Series, where he finished ninth in points and scored a victory at Pikes Peak Raceway.

His best NASCAR Nextel Cup finish of the season was a third in the season-opening Daytona 500.

Of his impressive run, Wimmer said, "We started making some changes. I could really feel them, kind of settled in and just stayed up front and tried to stay out of trouble as best we could."

Rookie Scott Wimmer wheels the yellow-and-black Bill Davis Racing Dodge en route to a strong finish. His best thus far was a third in the season opening Daytona 500 in February 2004.

NASCAR NEXTEL Cup Career Statistics

YEAR	RACES	WINS	TOP 5S	TOP 10S	POLES	TOTAL POINTS	FINAL STANDING	WINNINGS
2004	35	0	1	2	0	3,198	27th	$3,675,880

INDEX